TABLE OF CONTENTS

BIOGRAPHY

What is it about computer animation that makes a person want to pursue a career in this field? A half-interested furnace repairman once asked me what exactly it was that I did for a living. After several attempts at explaining computer animation to him, he finally responded, "so... you make cartoons!" "Yeah," I said, finally giving up, "Yeah, I make cartoons." Certainly, most people are not aware of what the term "computer animator" means. Here in central Ohio, it doesn't rank as one of the most well-known career choices. I think people hear the words "computer animator" but think the words "computer repairman" or "software programmer" or perhaps, just "geek." I'm actually happy that "cartoon-maker" gets on the list occasionally. Fortunately though, I love what I do. So any inconvenience experienced by repeatedly having to explain what I do is unimportant. This love for the work, of course, is the main reason why any of us become computer animators. We are instinctively drawn to it. It is not merely an interest or a hobby, but a passion.

For me, computer animation seemed to be an attraction that developed naturally over time. I didn't immediately know that I wanted to become a computer animator (there was no such career when I was younger), but I have always been interested in art. I have been making drawings and doodles for as long as I can remember. This attraction to drawing eventually expanded to become an attraction to painting and then sculpture, then to photography and filmmaking, and eventually even to stop-motion animation using an old super-8 film camera. Actually, the camera was new when it was first purchased back in the late 1970's. The term "super-8 film camera" just seems ancient to me now. So does the term "late 1970's" for that matter. Anyway, my interest in animation grew from that point. I didn't have my first experience with an actual computer until I was in high school. I didn't think much of computers at first. It was only when I learned that I could "draw" with one that my interest grew. I also learned that making a computer "draw," in those days, was an intensely tedious procedure. The Radio Shack Model I computers we used in high school certainly had their limitations, but I still tinkered with them occasionally. It was around that time that I saw on television a primitive wireframe computer animation, which captivated me. The animation showed a simple, three-dimensional house and a windmill with rotating sails next to it, around which the camera revolved to create a simple looping sequence. The animation was broadcast on a news program, the name of which I don't recall, but I remember looking at that simple animation and thinking to myself about how powerful that visual was. Even though this was certainly a very primitive visual by today's standards, it was a three-dimensional representation of a real thing which "lived" in it's own world, yet did not truly exist. This fascinated me. This was one of my first glimpses of computer animation and virtual reality. As time passed, I began to see more increasingly complex examples of computer animation and virtual reality. Early arcade games began to feature polygonal 3D computer graphics, like Atari's Battlezone (1980). Some of the first films to feature computer animation, like TRON (1982) and The Last Starfighter (1984), also appeared on movie screens around that time. The computer generated sequences in these films, while still somewhat primitive, demonstrated that computers were capable tools in creating visual imagery; and that computer graphics was rapidly becoming more sophisticated with time. However, these films required enormous budgets and personal computers were still very limited, so I continued with my drawing, painting and filmmaking.

When I entered into college at The Ohio State University in 1983, I enrolled in the College of Fine Arts and chose to pursue a Drawing & Painting major. I did well with the degree, but found I was not completely happy. I enjoyed creating my artwork, and I felt my skill set was increasing; but I looked at the art world at that time, too, and thought it resembled some kind of bizarre alien planet. I was pretty sure I didn't want to live on that alien planet, but I wondered if there might be another planet that was right for me. When I discovered OSU was beginning to offer classes to undergraduates in computer graphics, it at least sounded like the right solar system, so I checked into it. This was in my sophomore year.

Not surprisingly, I soon found that this direction was ultimately the right choice for me. After all, I have been a computer animator for the last 15 years. So, after a couple of computer graphics courses at OSU, I decided to change my major. Unfortunately, a computer graphics major did not exist at that time, so it became necessary to "design" a major. Fortunately, OSU was willing to let me do this. The Personalized Study Program that I developed was based roughly on the Drawing & Painting major that I had already started, so at least those classes didn't have to go to waste. However, added to that were several photography, videography, and cel animation courses, as well as several courses in advanced mathematics, computer science and, of course, computer graphics. Once the program was approved, I dove into it enthusiastically. I was especially enthusiastic about the computer graphics courses I was able to take, though there were very few of those available yet. The undergraduate program was still being developed then, so when each new course was introduced, I was one of the first guinea pigs to volunteer for it.

The computer graphics industry was still a field in its infancy at that time, so I didn't have an ironclad guarantee that there would be a job waiting there for me once I completed my studies. I still felt I had better options with computer graphics than I did with painting or sculpting, though, and the computer classes would at least make me more marketable. I also had two other factors working in my favor here in Columbus, Ohio. The first was that OSU had (and still has) one of the finest computer graphics master's degree programs in the world at their Advanced Computing Center for the Arts and Design (ACCAD). The second was the fact that one of the largest computer graphics production companies in the world at the time, was also located here – Cranston Csuri Productions. Incredibly, when I first made my decision to get involved with computer graphics at OSU, I didn't know either of these two facts. It was basically a fortunate twist of fate that I happened to stumble into the right place at the right time. When I did discover these other two facts, I felt my future plans had been clearly laid out before me, and I became even more confident about my decision. Those future plans began to solidify for me at the end of my junior year in college, when I was able to land a part time position as a film recorder operator at Cranston Csuri Productions. That was the summer of 1986.

My job at Cranston Csuri was fairly simple. I operated a machine which recorded digital images to 4"x5" transparency film. The animators of Cranston Csuri created these images from projects they were doing at the time, and the images were then used for client approvals, publicity stills, and other purposes. I became proficient with the machine fairly soon, and I began to develop good relations with the animators working there. It was also my good fortune to discover that Cranston Csuri Productions was located in the same building with the masters' program in computer graphics at OSU, so forming good relations with those in the masters' program happened naturally as well. By the time I entered into my senior year in college, I felt I was on the right track, and in a great position to achieve my goals.

All the pieces of the puzzle were falling into place. I was doing very well with my degree. My work at Cranston Csuri eventually expanded beyond operating the film recorder, and I was gradually able to become more involved with the actual production of computer animation. This was the beginning of my career as a computer animator. By the end of my senior year, I had been accepted into the master's program, and I had a few simple computer animated logos under my belt from my work at Cranston Csuri. It was then that I was presented with yet another opportunity, and a difficult decision.

One of the animators at Cranston Csuri was also heavily involved with Scoreboard Operations at the Ohio State University. In fact, he was one of the two original scoreboard staff members, and he was responsible for creating a great number of the original animations that were played on the OSU stadium scoreboard. He encouraged me to consider applying for a job on the scoreboard staff. This essentially part-time job would not only cover my tuition, but also offer me a monthly income. This created a small dilemma for me, because I felt my future was really with Cranston Csuri Productions. Financially, however, the scoreboard job was a much better opportunity, and it allowed me more independence. After some convincing, I decided to apply for the scoreboard job. When I was eventually offered the position, I decided to take it. It was difficult for me to resign from my position at Cranston Csuri, but I made it known that I ultimately wanted to return, and I left on good terms. In September of 1987, I began my work at the OSU scoreboard. At the same time, I began my studies at ACCAD.

About one month later, much to my surprise, Cranston Csuri Productions went out of business! I was completely stunned, as were most of their employees at the time. I saw a big part of my future evaporate into thin air that day. I remember having serious doubts about remaining in the field of computer animation. I also began to feel that being self-employed might offer better job security. Still, I couldn't imagine a better career choice for my interests, so I cautiously continued with my plan.

At least I had a job, and that helped quite a bit. I would have had a very difficult time continuing my studies at ACCAD without it, and the OSU scoreboard eventually became one of my favorite places to work. While the scoreboard job involved more hand-drawn animation skills, it also involved the computer. Each page of hand-drawn animation was video-digitized into the computer and compiled into a sequence. There was computer software available to clean up the digitized frames and add some special effects. The programmers on the staff also added 3-D computer animated effects to the arsenal.

During the next two years, OSU added a color scoreboard that the staff also operated, the level of sophistication of the software rose dramatically thanks to some gifted programmers on the staff, and the OSU scoreboard won a national award for excellence for the visual work our staff produced.

During the same time, of course, I was also taking classes and pursuing my masters' degree at ACCAD. I believe that I acquired a much more comprehensive understanding of computer graphics while studying there. There were no commercial software packages available yet, so all of the software was proprietary, written by students and faculty. I wrote a few simple programs myself as I explored computer programming further, which gave me a more thorough understanding of how computer graphics worked mathematically. Other graduate courses enabled me to broaden my aesthetic and philosophical understanding of computer graphics, while production courses allowed me to pursue my artistic goals and gain more insight into the practical requirements of computer animation. The education I received through ACCAD gave me a deeper appreciation of the physical and metaphysical nature of my chosen medium. I remember this as one of the most exciting periods of my life. Not a day goes by that I don't use the knowledge that I gained there.

Though my studies at ACCAD would continue beyond those first two years, I chose to leave the OSU scoreboard staff at that time, with some reluctance. I also found the computer animation market had radically changed. No longer were there only a handful of very large animation production houses. Most of them had disappeared, and had been replaced by several smaller production companies running commercially available software. In June of 1989, I went to work for one of those companies, Creative Connections Video, Inc., also here in Columbus. They were using a Cubicomp system to create 3D animation, which was not the most user-friendly system out then. It took a little while to master, but eventually I was producing 3D computer animation on that system, and recalling many of the lessons I had learned at Cranston Csuri Productions two years earlier. Being the sole animator for the company was a different experience, as I had always worked with a staff of animators before, but I soon became comfortable with that role. Each new project offered unique challenges to learn new skills and to improve old ones. After two years, I felt comfortable with my abilities, and started producing work that I could look at with pride. I had also learned something about running a business, though not nearly enough. Unfortunately, by August of 1991, the writing was on the wall – Creative Connections was going to close its doors.

This cemented my notion that self-employment was the only way to financial security in this business, and so I took what money I had, borrowed the rest, and purchased a computer graphics workstation. While I continued to look for a full-time job in computer graphics, I started looking for clients as well. When Creative Connections shut down in October of 1991, I was unemployed, but at least had some hope for a future. I began to do some freelance work out of my apartment. By January of 1992, with the help of a part-time job, a single client and a shared, rent-free office space, I officially launched Blak Boxx Computer Graphics. Because starting a company required an enormous commitment of time, I also made the difficult decision to end my studies at ACCAD. By the end of 1992, Blak Boxx had become my full-time job and was paying all my bills.

That was over ten years ago. Since that time there have been major improvements in the workflow of computer graphics production. Hardware and software have become increasingly faster and more powerful. Animations which once took weeks to render, now can be finished in hours, and with greater visual complexity. Recording animation to videotape was once a tedious frame-by-frame operation, which could consume an entire day. Now it occurs in real time, but in addition to videotape, I can record to digital disk formats or send frames over the internet. Blak Boxx has also changed quite a bit in that time. I started out with one client and very little business experience, learning everything as I went. In the past ten years, though, I have worked with close to a hundred clients, many of which I happily continue to call my clients thanks to repeat business and good relationships. My business experience has grown as well, but I still continue to learn as I go.

CURRENT POSITIONS AND RESPONSIBILITIES

To make a long story short, I do everything. I manage the business, I market and sell the company services, I create the product, I hire and manage employees and freelancers when necessary, I do the bookkeeping and I take out the trash. It breaks down like this. Managing the business involves keeping my hardware and software current and functional (not always the easiest task), and attempting to stay up to date on the latest developments in my field. I evaluate new software and hardware, and make purchases when needed. I open and close the "store," I answer phone calls and field questions from clients and vendors alike. I check progress on current projects and I make sure that projects stay on track to meet due dates and client budgets. I research and evaluate insurance, business leases, phone services, shipping and courier services and other vendor products in an attempt to keep costs down. I also purchase any office supplies and day-to-day items that are needed.

When marketing and selling my services, I create demo reels of my work, I make sales calls, and I maintain client relationships via email, phone, fax and meetings. I maintain a database of client contact information. I schedule meetings, create and distribute promotional items, write and submit press releases, and I create and maintain the company website. If any part of my job responsibilities suffers from neglect, it is probably marketing and sales, but I'm getting a little better at it. Fortunately, most of my business comes from word-of-mouth and repeat business. However, no business can afford to become complacent about this.

When creating "the product" my responsibilities include generating original concepts, storyboarding of concepts, creating estimates for each project, and keeping track of hours. I use several programs to do my work, including Lightwave 3D, After Effects, Photoshop, Illustrator, Adobe GoLive and Adobe LiveMotion. Choosing which software(s) to use to produce each project is part of the process, and then determining the best solution to use within that software follows. It is also important to determine the delivery medium, whether it is an animation recorded to videotape or any number of digital file solutions. If I have too many projects to simultaneously produce, I will also hire freelance help and will bring them in to discuss the job and get rates. Once a budget, concept and delivery medium is determined, I create 3D models, 2D textures, text, characters, environments, props and whatever other virtual requirements the project has. I compose, choreograph, and set keyframes for the project. I incorporate whatever effects, plugins, and scripts may be appropriate. Occasionally, I will also work on the audio for the project as well. I create test stills and/or low-resolution motion tests for client approval. Once tests are submitted, corrected if necessary, and approved, I render the final project and convert it to its final delivery form.

Then I arrange for the product to be delivered to the client for final approval.

Once everything is approved, then comes invoicing, which is part of the bookkeeping process. Having client databases helps to automate some parts of this process. I keep track of income and expenses, I deposit checks and I pay bills. I keep track of sales tax, mileage on my car and equipment changes for insurance and property tax purposes. I have to submit quarterly estimated income tax payments, workers' comp forms, federal payroll tax forms and various other government-required forms and returns throughout the year. Fortunately, I have an accountant to remind me of what is due and when. My accountant also handles my quarterly financial statements and year-end tax requirements. I'm probably forgetting something here, since this is not my favorite part of the job.

Oh yeah, I also take out the trash, which basically means that I try to keep my office and my computers reasonably clean. I do file management to make sure my hard drives don't get too filled up with projects. I record job information and backup project files. I also change light bulbs and dust and do all the other menial tasks that hopefully I will have a robot to do some day. Hey, one can dream.

Of course, I don't perform all of the above responsibilities every single day, and many of these items I have done so many times that they don't require much additional thought, but these are all responsibilities I have as a studio owner. I basically have to prioritize on a day-to-day basis. Anyone thinking about getting into business for himself/herself should take these things into serious consideration before making the leap. One of the great things about being self-employed is the freedom to choose what to work on and when, but even that has limits. One of the greatest drawbacks is that you don't get to spend as much time doing the part of the job that you love the most. Then again, sometimes a change of pace can be a good thing.

RÉSUMÉ

WORK RECORD

JAN. 1992 – PRESENT

Owner and operator of Blak Boxx Computer Graphics, a company that specializes in computer graphics, design, special effects and animation for video, film, interactive, web, and DVD applications. The company serves clients in the broadcast, educational, entertainment, retail and manufacturing industries.

Hardware: Includes dual-Pentium based workstations, printers, scanners and essential office equipment.

Software: 3D animation, 2D animation, illustration, effects and compositing, and web design, Windows NT/2000.

JUN. 1989 – OCT. 1991

Senior animator and computer graphics artist for Creative Connections Video, Inc. Work involved generation of 2D and 3D computer-rendered and hand-rendered animation and stills. Other responsibilities included

creation of corporate demo videos, and animation client relations.

Hardware: Cubicomp Picturemaker (IBM 80386).

Software: Paint and 3D animation, MS-DOS, REXX.

SEP. 1987 – JUN. 1989

Animator and operator for OSU Scoreboard Operations – Dept. of Athletics, the Ohio State University. Work involved generation of hand-drawn character animation and computer animation for display on a sports-oriented scoreboard system. Other responsibilities included game day operation of the board, coordination and creation of scoreboard sponsor animations, and production of an annual scoreboard demo video.

Hardware/Software: All proprietary.

JUN. 1986 – SEP. 1987

Freelance animator and film recorder operator – Cranston Csuri Productions. Work involved generation of computer animation and stills in a production environment. This work also involved photographing 4"x5" transparencies of computer animation frames.

Hardware: Vax 11/750, Vax 11/780, Sun 2 computers, 3D & 2D digitizers, PS 300 & Megatek vector display systems, Celco film recorder.

Software: Various proprietary 3D and 2D programs, UNIX, C, SunWindows.

SCHOLASTIC RECORD

Jun. 1987 – Jan. 1992: Studied Computer Graphics at the Ohio State University's Advanced Computing Center for the Arts and Design (ACCAD).

Jun. 1987: Received Bachelor of Fine Arts Degree from the Ohio State University, Summa Cum Laude. Major was a Personalized Study Program titled "Computer Graphics," emphasizing a blend of painting, drawing, computer science, film animation, video and mathematics.

HONORS

Oct. 1994: Blak Boxx Computer Graphics awarded "Chris" Award (best in category) for "1994 Animation Demo Reel," presented at the 42nd Annual Columbus International Film & Video Festival.

Oct. 1992: Blak Boxx Computer Graphics awarded "Chris" Award (best in category) for "1992 Animation Demo Reel," presented at the 40th Annual Columbus International Film & Video Festival.

Oct. 1991: Creative Connections Video Inc. awarded Bronze Plaque Award for "Creative Connections

Animation Demo 1991," presented at the 39th Annual Columbus International Film & Video Festival.

Feb. 1989: OSU Scoreboard Operations awarded 2 "Golden Matrix" Awards (best in the industry) for its "1989 Demo Video," presented by the Information Display and Entertainment Association (IDEA).

OUTER ENTRYWAY TO THE MAGIC BOX / PMG / BLAK BOXX OFFICES

Day 1 | **MAY 1**

PREDICTIONS

· *Render 13 animations for Wendy's marketing calendar project.*

· *Look into health insurance.*

· *Check on progress of promotional T-shirts.*

DIARY

I woke up this morning from the first sleep I have had

after working 39 hours straight on a project for Wendy's

RECEPTION AREA FOR OUR OFFICES. STRAIGHT AHEAD IS THE BLAK BOXX OFFICE. TO THE LEFT IS PMG. TO THE RIGHT IS MAGIC BOX.

MARK MITCHELL OF MAGIC BOX EDITORIAL WORKING AT HIS AVID DS EDIT SYSTEM.

International. The project is an animated marketing calendar, created with After Effects, which Wendy's intends to present as part of a large corporate meeting. The marketing calendar contains all of their marketing programs for the year. I can't really go into more details about it; because it's contents are carefully guarded secrets at Wendy's. Yes, I'm sorry, but I would have to kill you if I told you about it.

I started the rendering early this morning. I have to "baby-sit" the project, though, because I need to manually start the next animation after the current one finishes; and I don't have any time to waste. There is probably a way to automate the process, but I don't usually render several different animations in one day, so I haven't really researched it. I have to check each animation after it renders, anyway, to make sure there are no mistakes.

While the machines are rendering a long animation, I can fill you in on what's been happening lately. For the past four years, Blak Boxx has been co-located with two other companies, Magic Box Editorial and PMG Video Communications. Magic Box Editorial, run by Mark Mitchell, offers high-end video editing services, and PMG Video, run by Pat and Steve Gibson, offers video and interactive media production services. Between

PAT GIBSON OF
PMG VIDEO COMMUNICATIONS, INC.

our three companies, we can offer our clients the full range
of production services, but we can also offer individual pieces
to those clients who need only a part of the puzzle. Our three
companies do what we can to build each other's businesses, but
we also operate independently. Blak Boxx Computer Graphics is
currently enjoying a busy "spurt" of activity that will hopefully
continue for the rest of my working days. Sadly, that's not very
likely. Most often, my work level rises and falls much like a
roller coaster ride. The beginning of this year was more on the
slow side, because the economy has taken a downturn and

STEVE GIBSON OF
PMG VIDEO COMMUNICATIONS, INC.

the events of September 11th have finally caught up with small businesses like mine. This is not the best time for a slow year, because my wife and I are expecting our first baby in August. Because we're also expecting a lot of new bills, my income is more important than ever now. So, I'm grateful to be busy.

The machines continued to render, so I was essentially free to run short errands. I took my cell phone and headed over to check on the progress of some promotional T-shirts that I'm having made. Blak Boxx Computer Graphics is ten years old *this year, so I'm giving away the T-shirts to clients to celebrate. I discussed the artwork I designed with the owner of the silk-screening business where I'm having the shirts done. He had concerns that the artwork would not look bright enough printed in white ink on a black shirt, so we decided to have a test run for next Tuesday to see how the artwork translates into ink. While I was out, I decided to stop by the bank and deposit a check. I also received two calls. One was from my health insurance agent, and the other was a call from Brian of Wendy's International about a new project to be completed this week. This is turning into another busy week.*

After returning to the office, I checked the rendering progress and started rendering new animations. I called Brian at Wendy's to discuss the new project he mentioned on the phone. I turned out to be a simple project, but it needs to be completed by Friday morning. We scheduled an appointment for 4:15pm today to discuss it. A local producer and director, Michael Ivey, stopped by the office, so I talked with him a short while. I took a look at a commercial spot he directed, and we discussed the animation in it. Unfortunately, circumstances prevented him from using me for this spot, but I'm hopeful that we will work together on another commercial spot soon. Afterward, I paid some bills and tried to make sense of health insurance plans I have been discussing with my agent. My wife Rhonda and I are trying to save money where we can, and are hoping we can find a cheaper health insurance plan than what we have now.

I met with Brian at 4:15pm at Wendy's headquarters, which is not far from my office. What he needed was an interesting way to reveal text quotes for a tribute video being created to honor Dave Thomas. Dave Thomas, the founder of Wendy's International, had passed away earlier this year. Brian also wanted an animated title, and a lower third background element for text overlay. The meeting went fairly quickly, and I returned to the office to start new marketing calendar animations rendering.

Back at the office, Terry Burris of Burris Creative called to brainstorm a new spot for Time Warner Cable. We talked about a few different ideas and decided to let them incubate for a little while. I have six other projects on my plate right now in various stages of completion. The first is a website design for Everyday People Make a Difference, a service learning educational project. This has been an ongoing project. The second is a project for Aerosafe Inc., creating a set of exhibit boards for a legal case, also an ongoing project. The third is the Wendy's marketing calendar I'm currently rendering. Fourth is the project

I received today to produce animated transitions of quotes for the Dave Thomas tribute video. Fifth is a project for the Jack Nicklaus Museum, producing a video sequence of panoramic golf course stills with dissolves between them for a three-screen projection system. I just recently started this project for client, GC Films. Sixth is an animated logo for a company in Chicago called the Ramsborg Group, which I have not started yet. This is for a good friend's production company, Immersion Inc., also located in Chicago. The Time Warner spot will be the seventh item on my plate. I'm thinking about hiring a freelancer.

After starting new animations, I called my health insurance agent to schedule a meeting for tomorrow to discuss health plan options. I then began to search for appropriate fonts to use for the Dave Thomas tribute video, as I waited for the last animations to finish rendering on the marketing calendar project. Once the animations completed, I burned them on a CD to deliver to Wendy's tomorrow, then headed home for the night.

LESSONS/PROBLEMS

I was able to accomplish my goal today of completing the rendering for the marketing calendar project. I have learned to make the most of my free time while the machines are rendering, though, and so was able to accomplish my other goals, too. I have also learned that making T-shirts using white ink on a black fabric is a tricky process if there are any subtle gradations in the artwork. White ink is thicker than other inks, so it's not quite as good at creating subtleties or small details. I love black T-shirts, though, so I have to make the best of it. The only real problem I experienced today is fatigue. I still haven't recovered from that 39-hour stint from yesterday.

PREDICTIONS

- Finish the Dave Thomas tribute video quote animations.
- Review health insurance plans.
- Generate invoices.
- Make progress on the Jack Nicklaus Museum project.
- Call my lawyer about a will.
- Call Immersion Inc. about the Ramsborg logo.

DIARY

At 8 a.m. I drove to Wendy's to drop off the marketing calendar disk. They seemed very pleased with the look of the animation. I left after a short meeting with them. On the way to the office, I picked up a CD of images for the Jack Nicklaus Museum project. The images were scanned from slides and then burned to CD. I grabbed the slides and CD and drove to the office.

After going through email in the morning (mostly junk), I transferred the Jack Nicklaus Museum images from CD to my workstation hard drive, and then verified the images were correct by comparing them to a printout my client had provided. After that, I started on the Dave Thomas project.

I guessed this would be a relatively simple project. With the deadline being tomorrow, it had to be. I decided to dissolve on individual words of the quotes one-by-one, with a slight blur effect. I felt this would give the quotes more of a conversational speaking rhythm, more so than revealing the entire quote at once, and thereby give them a more personal quality. Dave Thomas was a very personable human being, so I thought this would be a good fit. I also spent more time trying to select appropriate fonts. It was somewhat difficult trying to find a font that was "friendly" yet also appropriate to the circumstances. I didn't want it to be too formal or boring, but it also couldn't be too casual or unusual. I wound up choosing a font that had thicker, more rounded serifs, with a slightly old-fashioned appearance. It seemed to fit both the circumstances and the man fairly well. All quotes by Dave Thomas were given this font, but the project also involved quotes by others, which described the kind of man he was. I chose a font with a somewhat more contemporary look for these quotes, to distinguish them from those by Dave Thomas. I also worked to create a lower third graphic to superimpose over individuals who had been interviewed for the video. Text will be placed over this graphic to identify the person speaking.

Over lunch, I called Holly Lockley at Immersion Inc. to discuss the Ramsborg Group logo. The Ramsborg Group specializes in meetings and staging presentations, so I proposed the idea of giving the logo a stage-like appearance with lighting effects. Holly seemed to be okay with the idea, but wanted a couple of storyboarded ideas to show the client, so that's my next task with this project. An interesting coincidence with Holly is that she and her husband Bob are expecting a baby too, with a due date about a week before ours. We wound up talking about baby stuff for part of the conversation too.

After lunch I continued working on the Dave Thomas project. For the title animation, I had the idea to add Dave Thomas' signature to it to make it feel more personal, too. I called Wendy's to find out if they had his signature captured as an image file. They said they did, but it would take a little time to find it.

At 2 p.m. I had a meeting with my health insurance agent. I had hoped this meeting would allow me to make a decision on whether to stay with our current plan or try something new. Health insurance for the self-employed is generally terrible. It's very expensive and provides little coverage. It's the worst of both worlds. Apparently the plan we have, which is through

Rhonda's work, is the best option we have. It's hard to believe, because the cost is fairly high, as is the deductible, but I suppose we're stuck with it. Although the meeting turned out to be something of a waste of my agent's time, she seemed to understand. At least it was a short meeting.

I continued work on the Dave Thomas project. Later that afternoon, I received a call from Wal at Wendy's with additions to the marketing calendar project. He needed to update the appearance of their soft drink cup and their French fry container with new flat artwork for a promotion they were doing. Actual containers had not yet been created, but they still needed to show what they would look like. The artwork would have to be three-dimensionally mapped onto photographs of actual containers. He would bring artwork and photographs over on disk later today.

I continued working on the Dave Thomas project, and around 6 p.m. Wal came by the office to drop off the disk with the new marketing calendar images. While he was here, he also helped me locate a Dave Thomas signature graphic that I could use for the title of the tribute video. I finished up working on the Dave Thomas animations later that evening, and burned a CD of the animations to deliver tomorrow. Afterward, I started work on the new marketing calendar graphics that were also due tomorrow, but later. I came home late, with a pretty good start on the additions.

LESSONS/PROBLEMS

Today, I did fairly well with my original goals. There was not enough time to call the lawyer or generate invoices or work much on the Jack Nicklaus project. However, there was a surprise thrown in with additions to the marketing calendar project as well. One thing that I have learned over the years is that you can never assume that a project is over. Occasionally, this will interfere with meeting deadlines for other projects, but I think I'm okay in this case. Overall, I felt good about what I accomplished, even though I did get home late. I haven't yet found a solution for avoiding that problem. Sometimes, one just has to stay late to get work done on time.

PREDICTIONS

· Finish the new marketing calendar animations.

· Start working on the Jack Nicklaus Museum project.

· Call my lawyer about a will.

· Generate invoices.

DIARY

At 8:10 a.m. I dropped off the Dave Thomas tribute animations disk at Wendy's. I talked briefly with people there, and then drove to the office.

At the office, I continued working on the marketing calendar additions. I used Lightwave to create the promotional cup image. I've included this sketch to illustrate that process. I attempted to use After Effects at first, but found the results were not as convincing. The cup involved a simple cylindrical texture map onto a 3D cylinder object, which was positioned to match the Wendy's cup in the original photograph Wal provided. The back of the cylinder was cut away so it would not render over parts of the original photograph that I wanted to keep. After lighting the object to match the photograph, I added a procedural texture to create the illusion of condensation on the cup for added realism, and then rendered a still. For the French *fry container, since it was a simpler, boxier shape, I used After Effects to position the sides of the promotional artwork into place. With After Effects' distortion tools, I was able to closely match the shape of the original box fairly quickly. This would have been a little more time consuming in Lightwave. After completing both stills, I created simple animations in After Effects to move them forward. I added a slightly springy motion to the items to give them a fun quality. I burned the finished animations to CD and drove them over to Wendy's around 11: 15 a.m.*

After dropping off the CD, I wound up sitting in on a meeting to review the entire marketing calendar video. It was a rare opportunity to get to see my work as part of a whole production, and there was a small change they wanted to make, so it was good that I was there. The change could interfere with working on the Jack Nicklaus Museum project, because the marketing calendar animations took a while to render; but it needed to be done today, so I had no choice. On the plus side, the Wendy's director of advertising was very pleased with the look of the marketing calendar. This is a very good thing.

At 12:00 p.m. I returned to the office and got some lunch and went through email. I had a lot of email to go through. At 1:

15 p.m. I started making the change to the marketing calendar animation, and by 1:30 p.m. I started rendering the change.

At 2:00, while my computers rendered, I decided to work on a personal project – a gift for my sister-in-law (also expecting) for her baby shower tonight. I scanned photos, resized them, and printed them out for a baby photo album. After that, I called my lawyer to discuss getting a will. With a kid on the way, my wife and I figured now would be a good time to look into it. My lawyer said that in Ohio, when you die, your belongings automatically go to your spouse, so until the baby is born there isn't really much of a reason to create a will. He did give me a lot of information, though. He said to call again after the baby was born, to set up things like trust funds and guardianships and so on. After hanging up with the lawyer, I scanned over a new issue of Computer Graphics World, and then I balanced my checkbooks. With funds as tight as they have been lately, I find myself balancing my check registry with online information fairly often.

At 4:30 p.m. the marketing calendar changes had finished rendering. I burned a CD and took it over to Wendy's; but first I stopped by my wife's workplace to drop off the baby photos I had made, since she was going to the baby shower tonight.

While I was at Wendy's, Wal asked me to work on a short project for the marketing calendar for him on their After Effects workstation. I was able to finish it fairly quickly, and then I drove back to the office. At 5:30 p.m. I arrived at the office and shut everything down to leave for the night.

Diagram sketch showing how promotional cup graphic was created for Wendy's marketing calendar project

LESSONS/PROBLEMS

I didn't get to the Jack Nicklaus project today, again, but perhaps I can work on it over the weekend to catch up. I also did not get around to invoicing, but again, there were

changes to do for the marketing calendar project. I'm glad that I accomplished my other goals, though. I did learn with the promotional cup graphic, that if you're looking for a three-dimensional effect, sometimes it is best to use a program that specializes in 3-D.

PREDICTIONS

· Get the Jack Nicklaus Museum project started!
· Work on invoicing.

DIARY

At 8:45 a.m. I came into work and sifted through a weekend's worth of e(junk)mail. Over the weekend, I decided that I needed to take a break from work and spend some time with my wife, so I didn't wind up working on the Jack Nicklaus project. It was a nice weekend, though I felt slightly guilty. One interesting thing that happened over the weekend was that a friend of mine, who is a movie critic, asked me if I would be interested in seeing a sneak preview of the new Star Wars movie, Attack of the Clones. Of course, I said yes, even though it would happen during the day on Tuesday. I may have to work late again tonight.

At 9:45 a.m. I started work on the Jack Nicklaus project, which involves a three-screen projection system. Basically it's just a series of dissolves (a slideshow, really), except that the images stretch across three screens, using three separate digital video projectors. The 54 images that I had on disk would ultimately wind up being 18, three-screen panoramas. The photographs that represented the left, center and right portions of the panoramas needed to be aligned and color-corrected so that their features matched to create one seamless image. Presented in a sequence, the 18 panoramas would reveal a time-lapse view of a golf course over the period of one year. I assumed that the edges of the photographs would basically line up with the edges of the video projection screens, so I figured this would be a relatively quick After Effects project. I knew that rendering would take up a few gigabytes of hard disk space, though, as the finished sequence would be about a minute and a half long for each screen.

At 12:00 p.m. Brian at Wendy's called with a fix needed for the Dave Thomas tribute animations. I was able to fix the problem quickly and begin re-rendering those animations over lunch. I burned a new CD and dropped it off for Brian.

After lunch, I continued working on the Jack Nicklaus project. My assumption about the seams of the photographs matching the edges of the video screens turned out to be wrong. The width of the center photograph extended beyond the edges of the center video screen, creating very noticeable seams on the left and right screens. Making those seams disappear was going to be a much more time-consuming task than I earlier imagined. I tried downloading software from the internet to help automate (and speed up) the process of removing those seams, but I found that the software was actually removing image features as it attempted to blend the photographs together. This was unacceptable, so I had to bring the images into Photoshop to manually blend them together. I also discovered that the photographs were not very well aligned with each other, so they required some manipulation to rotate and scale them into proper orientation with one another. With some of the panoramas, there was also no overlap between the photographs, so I had to fill in the gaps with Photoshop's clone tool. Another challenge I faced was that from one panorama to the next, the camera position was slightly different; so I had to manipulate the photographs further to match the first panorama that I created. I quickly realized that I had seriously underestimated how much time this project would take to complete. It was definitely going to be another late night.

At 5:30 p.m. Brian at Wendy's called with a last minute addition to the Dave Thomas tribute video. I quickly created the new still he requested and then emailed it to him. A friend stopped over to visit for a little while, then Rhonda stopped by and we all talked for a bit before Rhonda and I went out for dinner. After dinner, I returned to work on the Jack Nicklaus Museum project. The progress continued slowly.

LESSONS/PROBLEMS

Today, I basically still met my goal of getting the Jack Nicklaus Museum project off the ground. I made more progress than I felt I did, but I had to work late again to do it. The assumptions I made about this project were off the mark, but this was a technique that I had not experimented with before. Basically, I wasn't completely aware of what I was getting into when I started this project, so this has been a learning experience. The next time I get a project like this, though, I'll be more familiar with the potential pitfalls, so I'll also know to budget for more time. One of the great things I've discovered about computer graphics is that each project can be completely different, with its own set of challenges. It makes life interesting, because I'm constantly problem solving and inventing new techniques. On the flip side of that coin, though, it makes computer graphics a more difficult medium for which to estimate time requirements. This has been an ongoing issue, and I'm not sure if there is a good solution for it. Most of the time, clients are fairly understanding when I explain this kind of situation to them. Occasionally, though, I will have a client who is not. When that happens, I usually have to take a loss on that project in the interest of client relations and protecting my company reputation; and then I try to estimate more carefully on the next project. GC Films turned out to be very understanding about the Jack Nicklaus Museum project, and I was very grateful for it. I will try to deal with my invoicing goal tomorrow.

PREDICTIONS

- Complete a test for the Jack Nicklaus Museum project.
- Work on invoicing.
- Pay Bills.

DIARY

At 8:45 a.m. I went through another amazing bunch of email. Twenty out of twenty messages were strictly junk. That went quickly, at least. Reaching my goals today might be hindered somewhat by seeing Star Wars: Attack of the Clones. I'm not sure I'll get everything done. I have to admit a certain feeling of guilt about going to see it, but I still plan to go. It seems like a fun opportunity, and the effects in the previews look amazing. Occasionally, being self-employed has its benefits. This will be one of those times.

At 8:45 a.m. I began working on the Museum project again. Wal from Wendy's called to warn me of another impending revision to the Wendy's marketing calendar. He didn't have many details yet, though. Then it was back to the Museum project.

At 10:15 a.m. I left to join Scott Gowans, my film critic friend, downtown to preview the new Star Wars movie. It was a little longer than I thought it would be, but the effects were, indeed, amazing. I liked it better than the last one, but it still left something to be desired. I thought it was a fun flick, but I think the critics at the viewing almost universally despised it.

I checked my voicemail on the way back to work. Somehow, I had a message from yesterday, but had not received a page. Bruce from Aerosafe Inc. called regarding the legal exhibit boards project. That project was put on hold, because it looked like the case was going to be settled out of court. He let me know to go ahead and invoice for the work I had completed so far. Legal cases often work that way. It's not uncommon to work long hours to produce legal graphics that no one will ever see. I called Wal at Wendy's to find out if anything had been clarified on the revision for the marketing calendar project – not yet. I also called the office; there were no messages.

By 2:15 p.m. I was back at the office. That movie took a big chunk out of my day. I suppose it was worth it, though. I grabbed a quick lunch and started working on the Jack Nicklaus project again. Stitching the panoramas together continued to be a long and tedious process. By 8:00 p.m. I was finally ready to render a test of the project. I called the client to verify the sequence of the images first, and then I created a low-resolution test of the project to preview. The client would not be able to view the test until Thursday, though. That would at least give me some breathing room for tomorrow.

By 9:00 p.m. I decided to leave for home before my wife forgot what I looked like. I realized on the way home that the T-shirt shop was supposed to call me today. I will have to call them tomorrow. Also, the revision from Wendy's didn't materialize.

LESSONS/PROBLEMS

I was able to accomplish my goal today with the Jack Nicklaus project, though bill paying and invoice making continued to be neglected. It looked like I would be able to do that tomorrow, though. I probably had to work late today because of the movie in the middle of the day. Having fun sometimes comes at a price.

PREDICTIONS

· *Check on the status of promotional T-shirts.*

· *Work on invoicing.*

· *Pay Bills.*

· *Start storyboards for the Ramsborg Group project.*

· *Determine the best way to convert AVI sequences to MPEG2 files for the Jack Nicklaus Museum project.*

DIARY

I drove to work this morning with my wife Rhonda. I'm not quite sure if she recognized me, but she seemed happy that she didn't have to drive at least. I dropped her off at her work, and then went to my office.

At 9 a.m. I started paying bills. While doing this, I realized that I needed to work on first quarter materials for my accounting, so at 10 a.m. I started working on that. This is not the most exciting thing I get to do in my work, but it is one of those necessary things I have to do as a business owner.

At 11 a.m. Mark from Magic Box Editorial came into my office to show me materials on the Illusion particle system software. I spent a little time looking at their website and reviewing its capabilities. Lightwave 3D can do most of what I saw there, but the images were still impressive. Illusion might be a little easier to use for that specific purpose, though.

At 11:30 a.m. I took a break for lunch and looked over email. I received a notice that Lightwave 3D had been upgraded to version 7.5. I would have to study that later. At 12:30 p.m. I drove over to Rhonda's work and brought her back to my office. She needed to use one of my computers to work on getting college transcripts for her graduate studies. She took the car with her when she drove back to her job.

At 1 p.m. I started working on invoicing. I had about a half dozen invoices to send out. Work has been so busy lately that those were continually postponed. This is not a good thing. No invoicing means no income for me. I need to make this a higher priority. I realized while doing this that I also needed stamps.

Seeing the ten-year anniversary logo on the invoice reminded me that I needed to call about the promotional T-shirts. No one answered, so I left a message. I have been trying to integrate the anniversary logo into all of my printed materials, to build a brand identity for my company. I use the same logo in all of my communications – CD and video labels, mailing labels, letterhead, business cards, the company website, T-shirts (eventually) and even invoices. Branding is an important issue for any company, but it often gets overlooked for smaller companies like mine. I have attempted to maintain a consistent look to all of my materials, though, to build on name recognition and to advertise whenever I deliver a product.

At 3 p.m. I drove over to Aerosafe Inc. to drop off materials and an invoice for them. I also stopped by the post office to pick up stamps and mail other invoices. Still other invoices I hand delivered in order to make an appearance and visit with clients.

After returning to the office, I took a little time to review the new features of Lightwave 7.5. Although it is a free upgrade, I decided to postpone downloading it for now. Instead, I tested a process to convert the AVI sequences to MPEG2 files for the Jack Nicklaus Museum project. I decided to render the original sequences in AVI form to keep them free from compression artifacts. The digital projectors that would be used to present the sequences, though, required MPEG2 files. The conversion seems to be a somewhat tricky process. Later on, I began working on Ramsborg designs. Then Rhonda came by the office to pick me up, and we went home for the day.

LESSONS/PROBLEMS

Today was mostly what I would call an "administrative" day. Most of it was dedicated to paperwork – paying bills, making invoices and doing accounting work. I made decent progress on all of my goals. I was especially thankful to finally get invoicing done for now, as well as getting bills paid. Days like this would probably discourage some animators from becoming self-employed, because it can sometimes get a little boring. I don't mind getting a break from animation once in a while, though.

PREDICTIONS

· Set up a meeting to review the Jack Nicklaus Museum test with clients.

· Test AVI to MPEG2 conversion process.

· Work on Ramsborg Logo

DIARY

The day did not start off well. Our cat, Nikki, has been having medical problems lately, and this morning I had to take her to the vet to see what he could do for her. I am usually the one to handle issues like this, because my hours are more flexible than Rhonda's. Her job as a Kindergarten teacher has a stricter schedule. Her boss would have a problem with her showing up late and leaving fifteen energetic 5-year-olds unattended. Go figure. The vet scheduled another appointment for tomorrow morning to have an x-ray taken of the cat.

I set up a meeting at 10:45 a.m. for the Jack Nicklaus Museum project on my way home from the vet. After dropping off the cat, I headed straight to the office. At the office, I worked on first quarter accounting materials while waiting for the client to show up.

At 11:45 a.m. I met with the client from GC Films. A few
minor adjustments were made after viewing the test, one that
I recommended because one image seemed out of sequence
with the other images. Aside from that, though, the client
seemed to be very pleased with the results so far. I asked what
specifications would be required for the MPEG2 files I was
generating, and the client said he would get back to me on that.
After the meeting, I was able to make the changes fairly quickly.
At 12:15 p.m. I rendered the full resolution AVI files for the left,
right and center sequences.

At 12:20 p.m. I left to join Rhonda for lunch at her work. The
staff was having a potluck lunch today. Having lunch with
a group of elementary school teachers is an interesting and
entertaining experience. While I was out of the office I received
a voicemail from GC Films regarding the required specifications
for the MPEG2 files they needed me to generate. After lunch, I
returned to the office.

At 1:30 p.m. I attempted to convert the AVI files, but
experienced some early difficulties. The software I was using did
not seem to like what I gave it. All of my attempts to convert
the files resulted in the computer "hanging." I tried a different
route with a different piece of "shareware" software I found,

and I got fair results with that. I believed that the problem could be with the size I rendered the AVI's. MPEG2 files are in 720x480 (NTSC DV video) pixel resolution. I rendered the AVI's at 720x486 (NTSC D1 video) resolution by force of habit, because most of my clients request that resolution. I decided to re-render the AVI files at 720x480 and add a silent audio track to hopefully make the process of conversion a little more agreeable with the software. I made the changes and started the new render process.

I received an email from Terry Burris containing the rough script for the Time Warner spot. I gave Terry a call and we talked about the project a bit more. I introduced the idea of using animated television sets to carry the visuals for the introduction to the spot. He seemed to like that idea. Since Terry will be editing the spot at Magic Box editorial, I went down the hall to talk with Mark about the project and do some brainstorming. We came up with the idea of giving the television sets unique personalities to represent different types of tastes and wants that viewers would have relating to cable television. The TV's could then be placed in different environments that further reflected their individual personalities. I tried to come up with a rough storyboard concept to fit the script, and then I researched different television designs on the internet for inspiration.

When the Jack Nicklaus AVI's finally finished, I started working on the conversion process again. Unfortunately, I ran into the same problems I had before. Changing the resolution of the file didn't seem to help much. It was already getting late, but I felt compelled to figure this problem out before I left work. Rhonda was not especially happy with me. At least I was able to see her for lunch.

At 10 p.m. I decided to pack up my things and head home. I left very late, and very frustrated. The MPEG2 conversion process just does not seem to be working well using either of the two software packages I have at my disposal. Multiple attempts with multiple settings proved essentially fruitless. I am not in love with MPEG2.

LESSONS/PROBLEMS

I have encountered several problems with the Jack Nicklaus Museum project so far, because it involves a few procedures that I'm not that familiar with. Stitching together panoramic sequences was the first issue. Now creating workable MPEG2 files seems to be the second. MPEG2 files come in a variety of different "flavors" depending on the settings used to create them. MPEG hardware is also very picky about the settings, which are used to create the MPEG file, but each piece of hardware has its own requirements. I have discovered that while MPEG2 is a standard of sorts, it is a very loose and confusing standard. This project has definitely been a learning experience, albeit a frustrating one. I have to figure out some sort of solution to this problem soon. I do have to deal with deadlines, after all, and this project's deadline is approaching fast. I did not get around to working on the Ramsborg project, because of the other problems I encountered today. I'm also having a little bit of a mental block on that project right now. All things considered, this was not one of my favorite days. Hopefully, tomorrow will be a little better.

PREDICTIONS

· Finish Jack Nicklaus Museum MPEG2 conversions & deliver
CD to client.

· Work on Ramsborg storyboard ideas.

· Work on Time Warner Communications storyboard ideas.

· Take care of the cat.

· Work on first quarter materials.

DIARY

This morning I took Nikki, our cat, to the vet again to get her x-ray. I had hoped I would be able to bring her back with me, but I had to leave her there. I headed to the office, knowing that she would not be having a good day.

Once at the office, I received a call from the T-shirt shop. The owner had been out of town, so he was unable to return my call sooner. He had experienced other delays as well with computer problems, etc. The bottom line was that he would have a test for me to review on Monday, the 13th. Fortunately, I don't have any particular deadline for the T-shirts. I just need to hand them out some time this year. Hopefully, that won't be a problem.

I continued to work away at the MPEG conversion process on a smaller AVI that I used just for testing. Running the tests on the original AVI's – each one being about three gigabytes in size – was taking too long. Finally, by 12:00 p.m., I discovered what I believed to be decent settings for the conversion software. With that success, I started the conversion process for the larger AVI files. I took a break for lunch, and looked into getting a membership to Sam's Club online. The business membership seemed fairly reasonable, so I registered for it. With this membership, I could occasionally buy items for the office that I use fairly often, but also get the bulk baby stuff that my wife and I would definitely need soon. If not for the baby, I probably would not have considered it, but with the baby coming, it made a lot of sense.

By 2:30 p.m. the conversion had finished, and I burned a CD containing the finished MPEG2 files. I created labels for the CD, packaged it, and called a courier to deliver the package to the client. I then placed the package out by the front desk, where the courier could find it. Around 2:45 p.m. I started working on first quarter materials again.

Completing work on the first quarter materials didn't take very long. Once finished, I placed them in an envelope to deliver to my accountant. Then I balanced my checkbooks again and started working on the Ramsborg logo. I worked on several sketches, but didn't come up with any solid ideas. I think the frustration of the MPEG conversion process was still inhibiting my creativity somewhat.

At 5:30 p.m. I called the veterinarian about Nikki. The x-ray was helpful, but they wanted to keep her overnight to run some more tests. That's not what I wanted to hear. I'm sure the cat wasn't very happy about it either. I packed up materials for the Ramsborg logo and the Time Warner spot and headed home for the evening.

LESSONS/PROBLEMS

I am relieved that I finally discovered settings that seem to work for the MPEG2 conversion. I'm still a little wary about it, though, because of all of the unforeseen problems I have had with this project. I am being cautiously optimistic about it.

I am also glad to have completed the first quarter materials. Those are never all that fun, so it's good to have them done.

I didn't make much progress on the Ramsborg or Time Warner storyboards, however. I think I still have a mental block from the MPEG stress (and possibly cat stress too, I suppose). The

Time Warner concept is at least fairly well fleshed out. I just need to finish a good-looking storyboard to present. I will try to work on these over the weekend

FRONT DESK... WHERE CLIENTS ARE GREETED,
MAIL IS PICKED UP AND DELIVERED, AND
COURIER PICK-UP USUALLY TAKES PLACE.

PREDICTIONS

· Finish storyboards for the Time Warner "I Want More" spot.
· Work on storyboards for the Ramsborg Group logo.

DIARY

Over the weekend, I accomplished a few things. I brought home our cat Saturday morning. The vet placed her on a new medication for her problem. Hopefully, that will work out. I also delivered first quarter materials to my accountant later that day, and wound up visiting with him for a short while. I worked on sketches for storyboards for the Time Warner and Ramsborg projects later that evening.

When Monday morning came, having already made some progress, I decided to take some time to accomplish a few personal projects that had been postponed. I didn't get a chance to buy my wife something for Mother's Day yesterday, so I took care of that, and a few other items as well.

Once I arrived at the office, I went to work on storyboards. I finished black and white ink drawings for the Time Warner spot using my storyboard template. I then scanned the template, and finished colorizing the storyboards in Photoshop. I find this works better, because of its non-destructive nature. I can undo any mistakes easily, and I don't have to redraw any storyboard frames. I then brought these colorized boards into Adobe Illustrator to add text descriptions. The finished product winds up having a clean, professional look that way. I finished the storyboards around 3:00 p.m. The boards showed four television sets communicating four basic desires for the cable television viewer. I used some of the more interesting television designs from the past to give each set a unique personality, and then set each one in a different environment to enhance the scene. I thought the concept worked pretty well. I then saved and printed out the finished storyboards, and also exported JPEG files and emailed those to the client. I sent an estimate for cost along with the boards.

For the rest of the day, I worked on the Ramsborg storyboards. These storyboards would be generated differently from the Time Warner project. I made the decision to create still frames using After Effects for this project. The Ramsborg Group logo, because of its perfect circles and digital typefaces within the logo, turned out to be a complex logo to draw. By comparison, the Time Warner storyboards were fairly easy to draw, because of their organic, almost comic strip appearance. Even drawing just one frame for the Ramsborg logo was fairly time consuming, though,

Time Warner Cable "eye want more" storyboard sketch.

Time Warner Cable "eye want more" finished storyboard.

and I needed to create two separate ideas. By working in After Effects, I could make the storyboard images look great, and I could make progress on the production of the animation as well. There is some risk to producing storyboards this way, because the client may not like the idea. However, hand drawing the frames would take almost as long, they wouldn't look quite as nice, and the client might not like that idea either. I wrapped up work around 5:15 p.m. I realized that I did not hear from the T-shirt shop today, but I was too busy to deal with it anyway.

LESSONS/PROBLEMS

I found that these two projects required completely different approaches to developing their storyboards. The Time Warner project, because of its organic, almost cartoony nature, was much easier to draw by hand, then finish in the computer. The Ramsborg Group logo, on the other hand, involved digital typefaces and circles. Creating good looking 3-D text and circles by hand, with perspective and camera moves, is a time consuming process at best. Using software to assist in generating those frames, while a little risky, proved to be the better solution. These approaches also provided me with greater flexibility than traditional hand-drawn storyboards. I was pleased with the progress I made on both of these projects *today. Concepting these storyboards has been a little difficult for some reason.*

PREDICTIONS

· Work on Ramsborg storyboards.
· Look into T-shirts?

DIARY

A while ago, Mark from Magic Box Editorial offered to let me use a spare 21" monitor he had been using on his AVID DS system. It was black, so I was naturally interested, since my Dell workstation is also black. I have a dual monitor setup on my Dell, but one of the monitors is beige (i.e. not original equipment). At 8:45 this morning, I decided to take advantage of Mark's offer, so I could use the other monitor on the home computer. Unfortunately, changing monitors took much longer than it should have. I eventually discovered that my graphics adapter card would not work correctly unless I switched the order that the monitors plugged into the card. Why that worked, I don't know. Once I got it working, I thought the dual black monitors looked good, but it still seemed like too much time to spend on equipment aesthetics. Maybe the clients would like it. Who knows?

At 10:15 a.m. I received a call from the client for the Jack Nicklaus Museum project. Apparently the MPEG2 files that I

ME AT MY DELL WORKSTATION. IT LOOKS
A LITTLE BETTER WITH THE TWO BLACK
MONITORS

burned to CD were created at too high a bit rate, so their MPEG
hardware was having problems playing it. I was not happy to
hear this. The software I used told me that it had converted the
MPEG2 files with the correct bit rate. I looked online to see if an
update to my software existed. One did exist, so I downloaded
it and installed it. This software gave me a little more control
over the settings, so I experimented a while. Eventually, I
came upon a solution that seemed to work, so I started the
conversion process again.

At 2:30 p.m. I tried to squeeze in a little time to work on the Ramsborg animation design. The machines continued the conversion process, while I made some progress on the design work.

At 4:00 p.m. Mark from Magic Box came by my office with a problem. He was trying to import a sequence of image files into his DS video editing system, but the resulting sequences would not play back correctly. They looked jittery, like they were having a video field problem of some sort. I originally thought the fields had been reversed, but that was not the case. Reversing the fields to correct the problem only made it look worse. Then, I took a look at the image files and found the problem. The image files were in PAL video format, not NTSC. When the PAL format files were imported into the DS, the images shrunk vertically to match NTSC resolution, which messed up the fields. We found a workaround to the problem once we realized what it was. I went back to my office and found that the Jack Nicklaus conversion had finished.

At 4:15 p.m. Terry Burris called. The Time Warner storyboard that I sent had basically been approved with a few changes. Instead of using television set designs from the past, Time Warner wanted to use only contemporary or "cable-ready" television sets. They also didn't want to see antennas on their TV's. Other than that, they liked the concept, so that was pretty good news. I would get started on that tomorrow. In the meantime, I burned a new CD with MPEG2 sequences for the Jack Nicklaus project. I called the client to let them know that the CD was ready. They asked me to courier it tomorrow.

At 4:45 p.m. Hugh Rich of Visual Productions called about a potential training project using DVD. There could also be a few graphic elements required. He basically wanted to know if it could be done, and if we could do it. I told him that PMG Video and I could probably put that together. Then we talked about several other things. (Hugh is a friend that I have known for some time.)

At 5:15 p.m. I worked more on the Ramsborg logo animation design. I put together a concept using 3-D layers in After Effects that started to look pretty good. By 7:30, I had a finished design for idea #1 on the Ramsborg project. I created storyboard forms in Illustrator, printed out a hard copy for myself, and emailed a JPEG copy to Holly at Immersion Inc. to show to her client. I also sent her an estimate for that storyboard idea.

LESSONS/PROBLEMS

I learned that I shouldn't be overly consumed with the aesthetics of my equipment. It's nice to have your workstations look sleek and cohesive, but it has its limits, too. I also learned that MPEG2 is something I love even less today than I did before. I may need to resort to a different approach altogether if the test I created today doesn't work. I don't look forward to that, but if I am going to get into the business of producing MPEG2 files, I definitely need a different and more reliable approach.

On the positive side, I was given the green light to go ahead with the Time Warner storyboards. Also, it felt very good to make progress on the Ramsborg logo. I wish I had more time to work on it today, but I should be able to finish the other design tomorrow.

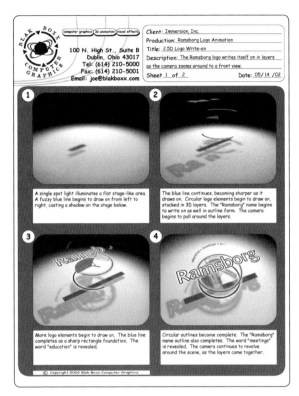

BLAK BOXX COMPUTER GRAPHICS

computer graphics • 3d animation • visual effects

100 N. High St., Suite B
Dublin, Ohio 43017
Tel: (614) 210-5000
Fax: (614) 210-5001
Email: joe@blakboxx.com

Client: Immersion, Inc.
Production: Ramsborg Logo Animation
Title: 2.5D Logo Write-on
Description: The Ramsborg logo writes itself on in layers as the camera zooms around to a front view.
Sheet 1 of 2   Date: 05/14/02

1. A single spot light illuminates a flat stage-like area. A fuzzy blue line begins to draw on from left to right, casting a shadow on the stage below.

2. The blue line continues, becoming sharper as it draws on. Circular logo elements begin to draw on, stacked in 3D layers. The "Ramsborg" name begins to write on as well in outline form. The camera begins to pull around the layers.

3. More logo elements begin to draw on. The blue line completes as a sharp rectangle foundation. The word "education" is revealed.

4. Circular outlines become complete. The "Ramsborg" name outline also completes. The word "meetings" is revealed. The camera continues to revolve around the scene, as the layers come together.

Ramsborg Group logo animation storyboard idea 1, page 1

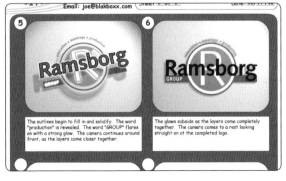

Email: joe@blakboxx.com   Sheet 2 of 2   Date: 05/14/02

5. The outlines begin to fill in and solidify. The word "production" is revealed. The word "GROUP" flares on with a strong glow. The camera continues around front, as the layers come closer together.

6. The glows subside as the layers come completely together. The camera comes to a rest looking straight on at the completed logo.

Ramsborg Group logo animation storyboard idea 1, page 2

PREDICTIONS

· Finish idea #2 for the Ramsborg Group logo project.
· Look into T-shirts?

DIARY

Rhonda and I drove together again this morning. After dropping her off at her work, I went shopping to get some things I needed for work, then I drove to the office.

At the office, I called a courier to pick up the CD for the Jack Nicklaus Museum project. At 10:15 a.m. I started working on the second Ramsborg concept. This concept would involve a little higher budget. I decided to use the "logo as a stage" idea I had developed earlier. I created 3-D models from Illustrator vector-based artwork and developed the lighting, surfacing and rough motion in Lightwave 3D.

At 11:00 I received a call regarding the Jack Nicklaus project. Apparently the new MPEG2 files were not working either. The bit rate was still off for some reason. Anyway, they recommended that I record the animations to Betacam SP videotape so that they could use their own encoder to create the MPEG2 files. I wish I had known about that before. I would

MAGIC BOX EDITORIAL'S AVID DS SUITE

have taken a different approach to the project. Now, I would need to involve Magic Box Editorial, because they own the Beta SP machines I would need to use. Unfortunately, there was nothing budgeted for Magic Box's services. I have a digital disk recorder of my own, which is connected to those machines, but it is only good for very short animations (under thirty seconds). So, I would have to transfer nine gigabytes worth of AVI files to Mark's machines over the computer network, in order for him to import them into his DS system for output to tape. That would take a while, and I needed to get this done today. Unfortunately,

Mark was out of the office right then, too. This would have to wait.

At 11:30 a.m. I took a break for lunch and caught up on email. At 12:30, I was back to working on the Ramsborg project. I continued to work on the lighting and effects in Lightwave. They were starting to look pretty good.

At 2:30, Terry called about the Time Warner spot. He wanted to try to make the TV spot match the print advertisement a little better. He emailed a PDF file of the print piece for me to view. It appeared to be a fairly different direction than what I was taking with the TV spot, but I thought it was still doable. We discussed ways to make the video more like the print piece without losing too much of the original concept. The print piece involved close-up photographs of people's faces instead of television sets. Those faces could be placed on the TV screens. Also the print piece involved a filmstrip graphic element that could be incorporated into the final TV spot. By the end of the conversation, we seemed to have a solution.

By 2:45 p.m. Mark was back in the office. I quickly informed him of the situation I was in. He was willing and able to help out, so I started copying the AVI's to his machines. After a long period of copying, we wound up with a problem. I was copying the files from Windows 2000, but Mark's DS system runs on Windows NT. Windows NT has a two-gigabyte file size limit, so copying the files to his system was not going to work. I would have to break up the AVI files. I was able to break up the files in about fifteen minutes by rendering six new AVI files using the original three. Now it was 3:30 p.m. and I started copying the smaller AVI files to Magic Box again. It was taking a very long time to copy such large files over the network, though.

By 5:00 p.m., it was becoming apparent that this solution was not going to work. Copying the files was still taking too long. Mark suggested that I provide him with the stills I created, so that he could then reassemble the sequence on his machine. Although I would rather not have forced this situation on him, especially with no money involved, in the interest of saving time I agreed to it. Next time around I will have put more in the budget for his time on similar projects. I collected the stills he would need and transferred them over to his machine.

While Mark went to work on reassembling the video sequences, I left to pick up Rhonda at work. On our way back to my office I could not hold back my frustrations with this project. Fortunately, Rhonda is a good listener, and she put up with all the venting that I unleashed in that car ride. After she dropped me off at my office, I thanked her for listening, and she drove home. When I walked back into the office, Mark was finishing up the video sequences and recording to Beta SP. I called the client at 5:30 p.m. to let them know that the tape was ready, but I realized then that I had no way to get it to them. The

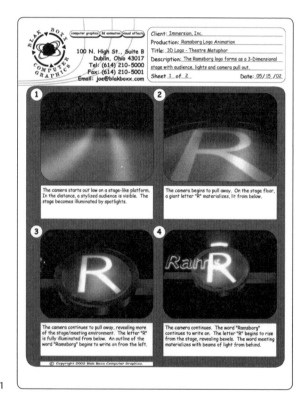

Ramsborg Group logo animation storyboard idea 2, page 1

couriers were closed for the day, and I had no car. They said that delivery by tomorrow morning would be okay.

After thanking Mark for all of his help with my emergency project, I returned to work on the Ramsborg project. I tweaked the lighting and effects for a while, before I finally came up

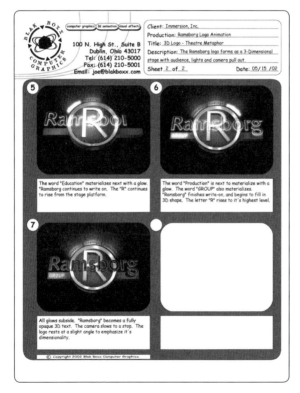

Ramsborg Group logo animation storyboard idea 2, page 2

with a finished design around 7:45 p.m. From there I created storyboards, rendered JPEG files and emailed them to Holly with an estimate. I also called Holly to let her know to check her emails.

Rhonda came back to the office to pick me up and brought dinner with her at 9:00 p.m. She is so good to me! While we ate, I tried to create labels for the Beta SP tape that Mark made for the Jack Nicklaus Museum. For some reason, my label software was missing the label templates that I created for Beta SP. Argh!! I spent some time creating new templates, while Rhonda patiently waited, and then printed them out. By the time I finished with that, I was more than ready to leave work.

LESSONS/PROBLEMS

Well, the fun never ends with the Jack Nicklaus Museum project! It was really nobody's fault, but this was basically a day from hell. It amazed me how many things went wrong and how many roadblocks I encountered today. I became extremely frustrated with this project, and worse yet, I added my burdens to people around me, like Mark and Rhonda. I was extremely grateful for all they did for me today. I am very fortunate to have such good people surrounding me. Somehow, with their help, each of the roadblocks was overcome, and I was able to say by the end of the day that all of the problems had been solved. I was even somehow able to complete the second set of storyboards for the Ramsborg project and deal with some issues concerning the Time Warner spot. One thing that I have learned is this – the next time that I have to create MPEG2 files for a client, I am automatically going straight to videotape. Then I will let someone else do the encoding. This process has consumed way too much time. Fortunately, I don't often have days like this. I do have days like this often enough to have a pretty good collection of stress toys, though. I suppose it was pure "luck" that this happened during the time that I was writing this diary. Hopefully, reading this will be beneficial to others.

BUG-EYED MARTIAN STRESS TOY EARNED ITS KEEP TODAY.

PREDICTIONS

· *Deliver CD to client for Jack Nicklaus Museum project.*
· *Deposit checks.*
· *Start production work on Time Warner spot.*

DIARY

At 8:30 this morning I drove the Jack Nicklaus Museum videotape to the client. I had hoped to be able to speak with the contact there, but they had not arrived at work yet. I deposited a couple of checks in the bank from Aerosafe and PMG, and then drove to the office.

By 9:30 a.m. I was at the office. I recorded the deposit in my checkbook, and went through email. I had received an email from a CCAD student regarding an internship. I have had interns work here before. These have always proved to be valuable experiences in the past, so I returned his email with a few questions. Hopefully, that will work out. Later, I balanced my checkbooks and paid some bills to help clear off the clutter on my desk.

At 11:00 a.m. I started working on the Time Warner spot. I started with an image asset search. For the faces, I was able to use the digital file Terry had emailed me of the print piece. I also was able to extract the filmstrip graphic from that. Then I started a search through my own image library for other visual elements. I found a couple of decent-looking television sets to use; one was even from a previous Time Warner spot. The four desires to be represented in the spot are "more romance," "more action," "more laughter," and "more for less." For the "romance" section, I did a search for flowers. I didn't have one image of a field of flowers that gave me the look I wanted, so I took individual flowers from several different images, and blended them together to create a more surreal-looking garden. I found a decent brick wall to use in the "laughter" section, representing the ubiquitous comedy club backdrop. I tweaked the color and image information somewhat to fit into the color schemes for each scene

Holly from Immersion Inc. called around 12:30 p.m. to verify that she had received the first storyboard for the Ramsborg project. I asked her to look for the second one as well, and to let me know which the client liked best. Afterward I continued on the Time Warner project.

By 1:30 p.m. I took a break for lunch. Over lunch I had a talk with Steve from PMG Video Communications about the

*possibilities of using DVD-based training. This pertained to the
project that Hugh Rich had mentioned a couple of days earlier.
I talked with Hugh and referred him to Steve to go over the
technicalities of using this approach.*

*After lunch, I continued with the image search. I found a usable
microphone for the "laughter" section and more television
images, which I was able to use after a little bit of clean-up
work. At 3:00, the owner of the T-shirt shop finally called
back to let me know that a test was ready to view. I scheduled
a meeting to stop by and see it at 8:30 tomorrow morning.
Afterward, it was more Time Warner image searching. Wading
through hundreds of images on CD-ROMS can take a while.*

*At 5:00 p.m. PMG Video had a test for an interactive DVD-
ROM. Steve had earlier found a good source for cheaper DVD-R
media, so we held off burning a DVD until the new media came
in. Afterward, I continued work on Time Warner. I located a bar
stool image for the "laughter" section and did a bit of image
manipulation with it to make it match the scene. Then I started
construction on the "romance" section and made good progress
there.*

By 7:00 p.m. the "romance" section was looking pretty good, so I decided to call it a night. I closed down the office and headed home.

LESSONS/PROBLEMS

Today was thankfully a much more productive and stress-free day than yesterday. I managed to meet all of my goals for the day and even enjoy my work again. The Time Warner project is turning out to be a fun project to work on. I feel like I have a good amount of creative control with it, and it's starting to come together nicely.

PREDICTIONS

· *Check on T-shirt test.*

· *Continue production work on Time Warner spot, and send a still of the "romance" section to the client for approval.*

DIARY

I drove to work with Rhonda again today. I dropped her off at work at 8:00 a.m. and then drove over to the T-shirt shop. At 8:30 a.m. I arrived at the T-shirt place and took a look at the test. The owner had silk-screened the artwork onto a piece of black fabric rather than an actual T-shirt, but it would still work. I thought it looked good. The concerns about the white ink not being bright enough were gone. If anything, the test came out a little too bright, but it still looked great. I told him to go ahead and finish the shirts. He said they would be finished, if not by later today, then by Monday at the latest. I left for the office after that.

By 9:30 a.m. I started working on the Time Warner spot again. I added text and moving filmstrips to the "romance" section. Mark from Magic Box stopped in to see how I was doing. After seeing my work he requested a full screen moving filmstrip for editing transitions. This was fairly easy to create. I worked through lunch.

The idea for the "romance" section of the spot was that the television set would start to swoon with the idea of finding more romance and then start floating in the air above a moving field of flowers. Tiny hearts would radiate outward from the TV and pop like bubbles. To the side of the TV, filmstrips would fly in with the words "I want more romance" to match the print piece. Time Warner changed the words to "eye want more romance," though, to make a clever reference to their "eye" logo. By 12: 30 p.m. I added the popping heart motions and tested the filmstrip motion. The filmstrips were moving a little too fast to be useful, so I slowed them down a bit and made another test.

At 1:45 p.m. I paid bills that were to go out with today's mail. By 2:00, I checked the new filmstrip test at a slower speed. It looked much better. Then I added motion to the flowers and finally to the TV set. Heart bubbles were then applied to the TV set afterward. Around 4:00 p.m. I rendered a test still and emailed it to Terry for approval. I continued work on the spot.

At 4:30 p.m. Rhonda called to let me know she was ready for me to pick her up. Terry Burris called shortly after that to talk about the test still. He liked the direction and the visual style that I was using for the spot quite a bit, and said that I should proceed with the rest of the spot.

After picking up Rhonda, I headed back to my office for a little while to squeeze in a little more work for the day. I started working on the "action" section around 5:30 p.m., and made a little progress there. At 5:45, Rhonda and I left to go to a family get-together at my brother Mike's house.

LESSONS/PROBLEMS

Today was another productive day. The Time Warner spot seems to be progressing well. The client likes the work. I'm continuing to enjoy working on that spot. It's starting to feel like a prospect for the demo reel, if I ever actually edit a new one together. The T-shirts are finally moving ahead, too. This was another good day.

PREDICTIONS

· Continue production work on Time Warner spot.
· Pick up some needed office supplies.

DIARY

At 8:30 a.m. I did some shopping to pick up the office supplies that I needed, including a new chair mat, and then I drove to work. At 9:00, I arrive at the office. I received a message that my accountant had called to let me know that my first quarter statements were completed. I replaced my sad and worn out chair mat with the new one, and then waded through a weekend's worth of email. Sixty-four out of seventy emails were junk, most of which were thankfully filtered directly into the trash folder. The others were mostly personal. One of the emails was from a friend warning of a new virus-infected file that should be deleted. I found the file on my machine, then had a feeling I should do some research on the internet. I discovered that the file was a normal system file, and that the virus warning was a hoax intended to get the reader to delete a needed system file from their computer. I emailed my friend back with the information, and then tried to clean some of the clutter out of my office. At 11:00 I worked on getting caught up on checkbooks for personal expenses.

At 11:45 a.m. I rendered a placeholder animation for the Time Warner "romance" section. Terry was going to start editing that project tomorrow, so I wanted to be able to complete as much as possible for that edit. He would not need the rest of the animation for a couple of days, and I was still waiting for footage that Time Warner was providing. After making the placeholder, I had some lunch.

At 12:15 p.m. I continued work on the "action" section of the spot. For that section, I envisioned a TV set jumping into the frame in a desolate landscape environment. The TV would "look" left then right quickly, and then jump off the screen in the opposite direction while jet planes soared overhead. The same moving filmstrips would reveal the words "I want more action." I began to do an image search to find a "desolate" environment. I found a few images that I thought would work, and combined them together to create the scene. I took a sky from one image, a flat, cracked earth ground from another, and distant mountains from a third image. Then I began to work on the motion. I had the filmstrips enter from the opposite side of the screen from the "romance" section, and reversed the direction of movement for the film sprocket holes. The filmstrip that would reveal the word "action" was given a more dramatic 3-D angle for effect. Then I began work on the TV motion. By 3:00p.m. I was able to start a test render.

While my workstation rendered, I took a trip to the banks to deposit checks. By the time I returned, the render had completed. I reviewed the animation, and decided it needed some further work.

At 4:45 p.m. I continued work on the "action" sequence. I refined the motion of the TV set, and added the background jet animations. These were basically just simple vector shapes with a motion blur effect. The jet trails were also vector shapes with a blur applied to the mask. The jets moved by quickly enough that the effect worked very well. By 6:45 p.m. the project was ready to render, so I started that and left for home.

LESSONS/PROBLEMS

Today was yet another productive day. There really weren't any major problems with the workday, today. The Time Warner project continues to progress nicely, and I am truthfully enjoying the work. I think I will be in good shape for the edit tomorrow. One lesson that I can share is something that I learned a while *ago concerning emails from friends. Any time someone sends me an email warning of a virus or of a special deal that seems too good to be true, I always verify it before I act. This has saved me a lot of time over the years. Most of these things are hoaxes. I try to educate about that whenever I can. A good site to use as a resource for verifying these things is http://urbanleg ends.miningco.com/.*

PREDICTIONS

· Complete Time Warner animations for edit.

DIARY

At 8:30 a.m. I arrived at the office and started work on the Time Warner spot. The "eye want more action" section looked good, so I started work on the "eye want more laughter" section. As I had previously done with the "action" section, I loaded the "romance" section project into After Effects, and then replaced the "romance" elements with the new project elements. The background image was changed from the field of flowers to the brick wall. The TV sets were exchanged. The face images, which were placed on the TV sets, were changed. Then I removed unneeded "romance" section elements and added the wooden stool and microphone image elements I needed for the "laughter" section. The moving filmstrips were basically right where I wanted them, so this process saved quite a bit of time.

I modified the motion to reveal the word "laughter" so it came in with a more "cartooney," springy move. I added similar reveal motions to the brick wall, stool and microphone as well. Then I worked on giving the TV set some life, to make it look *as though it was laughing. I probably spent the most time on this motion, since the TV set was a major focal point of the scene, and the laugh had to be convincing enough to "sell" the scene. Having the TV look like it was doing anything other than laughing would kill the scene, so I experimented with the motion until I felt it was convincing. At 11:30 a.m. I had the "laughter" scene pretty much where I wanted it to be, so I rendered it to disk and grabbed some lunch.*

By 12:00, I began work on the "eye want more for less" scene. I started with the "laughter" scene and changed out the elements again. I replaced the background with a plain white backdrop, and then replaced the television set and face image. In this section, I decided the have the final filmstrip appear on the TV screen itself, instead of having it outside the TV screen as it was with the previous sections. This gave the final scene a little more of a "hook" to grab the viewer's attention and sell the concept.

During the time I worked on the "for less" section, I received a call from GC Films regarding the Jack Nicklaus project. They were thrilled with how the time-lapse, panoramic sequence turned out when it was projected on the big screens. The client said to go ahead and invoice. I can't tell you how nice it was to hear some good news with that project. It was such a relief to know that all of that hard work and frustration had a good outcome.

At 2:15 p.m., just as the edit was getting started, I began rendering the "for less" section. I spent some time today going back and forth between the edit and my office to see how the animations were fitting into the edit and also to make quick changes to the project. One of the changes that I made was to re-render the "laughter" sequence in video fields, instead of frames, to make the motion a little smoother. The "laughter" sequence had the most movement of any of the sequences, so it seemed to benefit a little from that change. The other sequences looked fine rendered in full frames. The "for less" section rendered fairly quickly, and so I made that sequence available for importing then.

For the rest of the edit session, I remained available to discuss any problems and lend any help that was needed to help keep the commercial cohesive. Around 4:00 p.m. the decision was made to add another big screen to the end of the spot, so I quickly created a still with the screen cut out to use there. Where the hole was cut out, Mark could add whatever text he needed, place a logo, etc.

By 5:00 p.m., the spot was well on its way to being completed. The graphic elements were arranged and finished, at least, so I was able to leave work. I left to pick up Rhonda so we could visit with her brother and a friend of the family.

LESSONS/PROBLEMS

The Time Warner project seems to have come together in exactly the way that the Jack Nicklaus Museum project didn't. It helped that I was in comfortable territory, working in After Effects and producing image sequences that I knew would work on the equipment that Magic Box uses. Consequently, I could make more accurate assumptions based on previous experience, and the project seemed to flow much better and more smoothly. There were very few problems, and none were major.

One great thing about this particular project was that I was able to participate in the video editing process. This isn't something that I often get to do, because the client is rarely willing to pay for it. Since I was working on the animation simultaneously, though, the timing was perfect. It would be beneficial to be able to arrange for this to happen with future projects as well, at least for projects being edited at Magic Box.

Another big timesaver for this project was that four scenes in the project contained enough similarities that I was able to make use of work that I had done for previous scenes when I set up the later ones. Although this isn't always possible, I try to take advantage of previous work when I can.

PREDICTIONS

- Invoice for the Jack Nicklaus Museum project.
- Check the status of the Ramsborg storyboard approvals.
- Catch up on administrative work
- Take my car in for an oil change.

DIARY

Today will be a "catch up" day. The only problem with devoting all of my time to the production side of a project is that other necessary tasks get put off. Of course, I'm happiest when I'm working on production, but there are other factors to running a business that can't be ignored for long. Rhonda and I drove separately today, and I met her at the service station on the way to work. We dropped off my car for its oil change, and then I drove her to work. At 8:30 a.m. I arrived at the office and went through my email. I looked into the "U Promise" college saving plan for our "little one on the way," and decided to register for that. At 9:00 a.m. I called Holly to see if any decisions had been made about the Ramsborg storyboards. I left a message on her voicemail. Then I filled out some paperwork. Afterward, I called GC Films to let them know I still had their original slides and to arrange for them to be *picked up. They let me know the slides would be collected next Tuesday.*

At 10:00 a.m. I created an invoice for the Jack Nicklaus Museum project. I couldn't bill for all of the hours that I had put into it. There was a lot of time spent on the learning curve, so I tried to be fair about it. The client and I had earlier agreed to a modified figure, and I stayed with that.

At 12:15 p.m. I picked up Rhonda from work and drove to the service station to pick up my car. After that we had lunch together. It's nice when we can do that. It's one of the advantages of working five minutes from each other. After Rhonda drove back to work, the rest of the afternoon I worked on errands. At 1:00 p.m. I did some shopping for the office and for our house. At 2:15 p.m. I deposited a check. At 3:30 p.m. I visited my eye doctor for an appointment. At 4:00 p.m. I picked up first quarter materials from my accountant. I talked with him a little bit about property taxes this year. Later I went home. There have been a lot of personal projects that have been backing up, so I decided to work on those before Rhonda and I got into our evening plans. I also planned to take tomorrow off to catch up on work around the house that had been put off because of all the late nights I was previously at the office.

LESSONS/PROBLEMS

Today worked out pretty much the way I thought it would. I accomplished my goals and caught up on some administrative work during this "down" time between projects. I have to take advantage of these moments when I can. Sometimes, when I am especially busy at work, it can be several days or weeks before I can get back to personal or home projects, so there's a pile waiting for me at the next down time.

PREDICTIONS

· Work on promotional items – T-shirts, website, etc.

DIARY

Another good thing to do while in between projects is to spend some time working on marketing. As I've said before, this is one area that I need to work on more often. This morning I devoted some time to working on the website. I am working on developing more Macromedia Flash content to the site to demonstrate that capability. Being a computer animation company, having more movement on my website is also a good idea, so long as it has a purpose. Flash is a great way to accomplish that. I use Adobe's LiveMotion to create Flash animations, because it has more animation capabilities and more productivity enhancements than Flash. It also has an interface which is very similar to After Effects, with which I am completely comfortable; so I don't have to learn an entirely new interface logic and production routine to create my work.

At 10:00 a.m. I received some revisions to the Time Warner spot. The client wanted to see more of the face used on the TV set in the "romance" section. They felt that the woman's face used for that section needed to be made a bit more attractive.

I repositioned that face within the television screen area and also performed a little "plastic surgery" to remove some small wrinkles on her face and tone down her expression a little bit. Time Warner also wanted to replace the face in the "action" section with a short motion clip of their Road Runner character to advertise their high-speed internet cable service. I didn't feel that putting the Road Runner clip in the "action" section was aesthetically or logically the better choice, since every other scene used a face image within the television, but sometimes you have to do what the client wants. At least it was a desert scene, so the Road Runner character seemed at home in a way. The face image that had been chosen for the "action" section was also perhaps not the best face to communicate that quality, either. I was able to make both of the changes fairly quickly.

By 11:15 a.m. I had completed the changes to the Time Warner spot. Steve from PMG Video stopped in the office and asked me if I could burn a couple of DVD demos for them. They supplied the files over the computer network, and I burned the DVD's in the background. This is just another example of the kind of symbiotic relationship that our three companies have. Currently Blak Boxx Computer Graphics is the only one of our three companies with a DVD burner, so this is one way that I can help serve the other two companies that coexist here. We do small favors like this for each other all the time.

At 11:45 a.m. I received a call from the T-shirt shop. The T-shirts were just now being run. I don't know why it took a week to do, but at least they were getting started now. Fortunately, I was in no big hurry, so I didn't mind. The owner of the T-shirt shop also knew this, so I think he was taking care of bigger projects and emergencies first. Had I been in a greater hurry, I'm sure the shirts would not have been postponed so long.

At 12:00 p.m. I started working on the website again. I am trying to improve the looks of the services page and also add more visual examples and links there to show off what Blak Boxx can do.

At 1:00 p.m. I had lunch with Hugh Rich. We talked about a lot of things, but mainly discussed an upcoming infomercial that he will be doing, and what graphics might be needed for it.

At 2:30 p.m. I was back at the office, and I continued to work on the website. I also burned a few more DVD's for PMG Video.

At 6:15 p.m. I closed down the office and headed home for the weekend. It looked like I would be able to relax on this one.

LESSONS/PROBLEMS

Today I was able to focus on my goals fairly well. The only problem was that the goals were a little vague. In the future, I think it would be helpful to be more specific about the goals I want to accomplish. I was able to make some progress today, but I felt I could have accomplished more. For example, I need to spend some time to design specific Flash animations to add to the website. I find I am able to exploit the software better and learn its features faster if I have a specific project goal in mind. Other than that, the day went pretty well.

PREDICTIONS

- Apparently somewhere in the last few days I lost my driver's license, so I need to locate that ASAP.
- Create a DVD from video footage supplied by Magic Box Editorial.
- Call Immersion Inc. about the Ramsborg project.
- Check on promo T-shirts.

DIARY

I had a great long weekend for this past Memorial Day. It is a rare treat that I get to enjoy three days off work without having any pressing concerns about a current project. I really enjoyed it. The only downside was that on Saturday, I realized that I had lost my driver's license. This has never happened before, so I was a little nervous about it. The first part of my morning, then, was spent calling businesses that I had visited in the past few days in order to track the license down. Fortunately, I was able to determine fairly quickly that my bank had it. I'm not sure why they didn't bother to call me sooner, because I had left it there last Thursday when I deposited my check. I thought they could have called me that day or Friday or Saturday, but for some reason, they didn't. I wasn't too happy about that.

At 9:30 a.m. I called to get the video that I needed to get digitized for the DVD. I was told I would have it later today. I then checked my voicemail. I had received a call from Kathy at Everyday People Make a Difference. She had some concerns about navigation for the website interface that I had been designing. I loaded the interface screens into Photoshop to refresh myself on the project, and then I gave her a call at 10: 30 a.m. to set up an appointment. Her machine answered, so I left a message. Afterward, I called Holly at Immersion Inc. to talk about the Ramsborg project. The client had decided to go with the first idea, which, not surprisingly, also involved a lower budget. I told her that I would start on it and try to have the project finished by the end of the week. At 10:45 a.m. I called about the T-shirts. They were done and were ready to be picked up.

At 11:00 a.m. I took a break for lunch. I looked into sites by other web designers to see what they were doing and to get some inspiration. I also called the vet to see what to do next with our cat.

At 12:00 p.m. I started work on the Ramsborg animation. The nice thing about the process that I used to create the storyboards is that the production process had already been started. Of course, all of the work that went into producing the second set of boards was lost, but the whole process still seemed to work well for this project. Had I drawn the storyboards by hand, none of that time would have contributed toward the production process.

By 2:00 p.m. the video needed for the DVD had been digitized. This was basically just a set of three commercials that had already been recorded to professional videotape. The client wanted to also have a DVD copy of the videotape for his own records. The project would not pay much money, but this was an opportunity to create one of my first DVD's, aside from burning demos for PMG Video. The digitized video file was an AVI file located on Magic Box Editorial's machine. I had to copy this file over the network to my machine to do the DVD burn. We chose to work with an AVI file, because we thought we would provide better image quality for the DVD. Also DVD specifications for MPEG2 files are pretty well known, so making MPEG2 files for DVD is a less complicated process than the process I went through on the Jack Nicklaus project. Since the AVI file was taking a while to transfer over the network, I took this opportunity to visit the bank to collect my driver's license and also to deposit checks.

By 2:30 p.m. I was back at the office. I started working on transcoding the AVI to DVD MPEG2 using DVD authoring software. The AVI to DVD MPEG2 conversion was exceptionally slow. At this point I wondered if there might be a better method to doing this. I may need to upgrade to another software or get a real-time encoder later. At 3:45 p.m. the DVD transcode continued. I tried to get other things done in the meantime. I went through mail. I balanced checkbooks. I considered that I should speak to PMG Video about the MPEG issue. They have an MPEG digitizer, but I was a little concerned about the video quality.

By 5:00 p.m. the DVD transcode finally finished. I left to pick up Rhonda at work, and then came back to the office. By 5: 30 p.m. I had successfully burned the DVD. I checked the video on my computer and it seemed to look good. I packed it in my briefcase to test it on my home DVD player and television set. That night, on the home DVD system, I discovered what appeared to be video field problems.

LESSONS/PROBLEMS

Today I learned to keep a better eye on my bank and my driver's license. That was not a fun thing to worry about. It concerns me that my bank didn't tell me sooner that they had my license.

I'm discovering similar problems burning this DVD project that I had with the Jack Nicklaus Museum project, though not as severe. My promise to myself to always deliver MPEG2 files by providing videotape won't work here because the client already has a videotape but wants a DVD. This project is just different enough that I can't use the same lesson. The process is still taking too long, though. Perhaps using PMG will be the better way to go. Because it's my first experience on this kind of project, there's that learning curve again.

PREDICTIONS

· Fix the DVD problems discovered last night.
· Continue work on the Ramsborg logo.
· Pick up T-shirts.

DIARY

At 8:00 a.m. I was at the office going through email. I also
worked on a résumé design for my cousin to help make it
visually more effective and to trim down some of the text to
make it more readable.

At 10:00 a.m. I started working on the DVD issue. I believed
that the issue might be related to a similar issue I had earlier
with the Jack Nicklaus Museum project. I discovered that the
AVI files that Magic Box had created were digitized at NTSC
D1 (720x486) resolution, but MPEG2 files are at NTSC DV
(720x480) resolution, so when the AVI was converted to
MPEG2, the video was apparently scaled vertically and the
video fields were thrown off. This caused a harsh flickering
in parts of the video that contained a lot of movement, and
that was unacceptable. Rather than re-digitize the videotape
and produce a new AVI file, though, I decided to modify the
original AVI file in After Effects. I loaded the original AVI file,

and lined it up with the top edge of the frame, but I set the frame's resolution to DV resolution. This way, six scanlines at the bottom of the original AVI file would be removed when I rendered the new AVI. Since the new AVI would then be in DV resolution, the scaling issues and the video field flickering would be gone.

At 11:15 a.m. I created the new AVI using After Effects. I also simplified the DVD menu using DVD authoring software. At 11: 45 a.m. I started the process of transcoding the AVI into DVD MPEG2 again. This was a long process. I talked with Mark at Magic Box and with Steve at PMG, and we additionally decided to use PMG's real time MPEG2 encoder to encode directly from the original videotape, and then compare the times required. I also squeezed in some time for lunch.

By 12:00 p.m. it became extremely obvious that the real time encoding process was moving much quicker, and the resulting video quality was certainly acceptable for a copy of a videotape. Steve was also able to subdivide the incoming video further and separate the individual commercial spots into three MPEG2 files instead of having them all stuffed into one file. I abandoned the AVI to MPEG2 conversion that I was doing on my machine in favor of the files that PMG had produced. I also took some time to create a simple animation to place at the beginning of the DVD to promote Blak Boxx Computer Graphics. This was called a "first play movie" in DVD terminology.

At 2:00 p.m. the mail arrived. I received a welcome check from Wendy's International. They have always been good about paying on time. I also received a call from Geoff of Family Video Treasures. He had a new project for me to do. He stopped by later to drop off some CD's for me. A while ago, I created a reusable animation for Geoff to use in wedding videos that he produces. The animation involves several photographs, which float down into a photo album-like book. The animation is used as an introduction to the wedding videos that he creates for his clients. For each new wedding video that he makes, he supplies me with a new set of photographs that I can then "plug into" the animation, replacing the original photographs. It only takes about an hour or so of my time to produce, and his clients seem to really like the high-end look to their videos. It has been a good ongoing project for me and for Geoff.

The simple "first play" animation that I started earlier became much more complex. My thought was that if I'm going to create one, I might as well create a good one that I can use again. I continued to make progress on it, and by 3:30

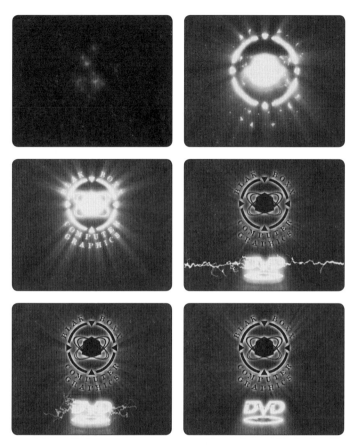

Blak Boxx Computer Graphics DVD "first play" animation

p.m. I rendered the animation to include on the DVD. I then developed the menu for the DVD a little more, again thinking that this would be something that I could reuse in the future.

At 4:00 p.m. I left to pick up Rhonda to take her to a meeting for postgraduate studies. While I was out, I stopped by the T-shirt shop to finally pick up my T-shirts. They looked great. They did seem just a little on the bright side, but I was pleased with how they turned out. I ran a few other errands and then picked up Rhonda from her meeting at 6:00 p.m. After dropping her off at home, I drove back to the office to continue work there.

By 7:00 p.m. I was back at the office to finish up my DVD work. I continued to work on the "first play" animation for a while. I adjusted the motion and the effects until I was happy with the results. I also added sound effects to give it a professional touch. I finished the DVD menu, and then burned the DVD. By 9:00 p.m. I was ready to go home. I took the DVD with me to test again on my home machine. This time there were no flicker issues, and the DVD looked much more impressive.

LESSONS/PROBLEMS

Today, admittedly, I got a little sidetracked. The DVD project turned out to be a much bigger monster than I originally had

BLAK BOXX COMPUTER GRAPHICS 10 YEAR
ANNIVERSARY T-SHIRT FRONT

T-SHIRT BACK

planned, but I managed to create some assets that I can use for all future DVD projects, including an eventual DVD demo for Blak Boxx Computer Graphics. It also looks like we discovered a good solution for creating DVD backups of client videotape projects. It took a while to work it out, but it seems to be a quick and reliable system. Creating my first DVD has been a lengthy experience, but it is also exciting to see it finished. The "first play" animation looks and sounds great.

Also today, I finally have my long-awaited promotional T-shirts. I can't wait to start handing them out. I don't know how much business they will create, but I imagine it will more than cover the cost of creating the T-shirts. Sometimes getting new business is just a matter of reminding people that you are there.

PREDICTIONS

- Work on Ramsborg logo.
- Deliver finished DVD.
- Timer permitting, start work on the Family Video Treasures projects.
- Deposit checks.
- Leave work early for prenatal doctor's appointment.

DIARY

Today I gave out the first promotional Blak Boxx T-shirts to people at the office. Of course, they were very happy to receive them. Everyone likes to get free T-shirts once in a while. I let Mark at Magic Box know that his DVD project was completed. Because it took so long to create, though, I told him there would be no charge for it. It was a valuable learning experience, at least. Next time around, it should be more profitable. While I talked with Mark, he asked me for a favor. His daughter would be getting married on June 1st, and he wanted me to scan some photographs for a reception video that he was creating. I told him that I would help out. At 11:00 a.m. I went through email. Then I worked on scanning photos for Mark, while I took some time to sneak in a lunch.

At 1:00 p.m. I went back to the "first play" animation to add a little padding in the front and back of the animation. I noticed on the first DVD that the animation started and ended a little too quickly, so I modified the animation for whenever I create my next DVD.

At 1:30 p.m. I continued work on the Ramsborg project. The animation was coming together, but I did not like how the animation was looking over the light gray background. I tried experimenting with a dark blue background similar to what I had used in the second storyboard design, and I found that I liked the look much better. I called Holly at Immersion Inc. to see if pursuing that direction would be okay with her and her client. I left a message on her voicemail.

At 4:00 p.m. I left work to pick up Rhonda for her doctor's appointment. We had to be on the other side of town by 4:30 p.m. so I had to leave work early.

LESSONS/PROBLEMS

My goals were basically met today. I was slightly delayed due to the scanning project for Mark, but I don't think it will be a big deal. I still have plenty of time to complete the projects I am working on for Immersion Inc. and Family Video Treasures.

Today was also a short day, so I didn't accomplish as much because of that. Tomorrow should be a better day.

PREDICTIONS

· Deposit checks.

· Pay bills.

· Work on Ramsborg project.

· Start work on the Family Video Treasures projects.

DIARY

I stopped by the bank on the way to work and deposited
checks. So, hey! That's one goal accomplished! I arrived at the
office later and started work on the Ramsborg project again. I
tried to reach Holly at Immersion Inc., but I got her voicemail
again. I decided to continue in the direction that I was going. If
nothing else, I could still use the motion that I was creating for
the animation and some of the effects work. I also had a feeling
that Holly would be okay with the change. I was not as sure
about her client, though.

At 12:00 p.m., Holly called back about the Ramsborg logo. She
said it should be fine and that she trusted my judgment. I told
her that I would try to complete the project today, and that I
thought the project was looking good.

I went back to work on the project. I added some animated

Ramsborg Group logo animation images

textures to the background layer and a few other layers of the logo to give it some added visual interest. I lengthened the animation to make the ending loopable and to add a fade up from black at the beginning. I also changed the timing of some of the layer motions to distribute them a little better.

At 3:00 p.m., Pat Gibson from PMG Video stopped into my office to talk about an update to an old project. PMG was in the process of creating a new marketing CD for the American Pavement Association (APA), and she wanted me to revise the design of a CD we had previously done for them. The idea was to make an entire series of CD's, so it was important to keep some of the design features from the first CD, but to make the new CD different enough to give it a look of its own. Pat dropped off some materials for me, and I told her I should have something for her by the middle of next week.

After the meeting, I continued to work on the Ramsborg project. By 4:15 p.m. I was able to render the project in After Effects. Afterward, I converted the animation to a QuickTime movie file. I also took some time to pay some bills. By 5:00 p.m. I was able to leave work to join Rhonda for a Friday night social gathering with her co-workers. I deposited checks on the way there.

LESSONS/PROBLEMS

Today I was able to be a bit more productive. The Ramsborg logo is basically completed. I just need to send it to Immersion Inc. in Chicago tomorrow. It is not typical that I would change the direction of the storyboards that I create. I make changes to other people's storyboards all the time, but not usually to mine. This was a little more than a simple background change, too, but the look of the animation was much improved. My goal is to try to find the best solution for my client. If that means that an original idea of mine can be improved, I will try to work in that direction. This change was purely a matter of improving the visual impact of the design. Yes, sometimes I "do it for the art." It's not always the best business decision, but I also have to satisfy my artistic side, too, to get some added enjoyment from my work. Pursuing this direction didn't really add that much extra time to the project anyway.

PREDICTIONS

- Ship the Ramsborg logo animation.
- Start work on the Family Video Treasures projects.
- Pay personal bills.

DIARY

The day started slowly. I was still recovering from a very busy weekend, and I was a little tired. I went through the weekend of email and spent some time deleting clutter from my inbox. I had close to a hundred messages that had been lingering there for a while. I managed to get that number reduced to about half. Later that morning, I decided that I had better check the appearance of the Ramsborg logo on an NTSC monitor to see if it still looked okay. To do that I would have to copy it to my digital disk recorder, which was also filled with clutter from previous projects. I took some time to find projects that I felt were safe to remove. By noon I was able to verify the look of the Ramsborg logo on an NTSC monitor. I thought it still looked good, so I burned a CD and took a lunch break.

At 1:00 p.m. I created a FedEx shipping package to send the Ramsborg CD to Holly in Chicago. I also included a note about the promo T-shirts. Since Holly was also expecting, I decided *not to ask about what size she wanted right now. That can be a touchy subject with pregnant women. I packaged the CD, prepared a shipping label, and then walked the finished package over to a nearby FedEx drop-off box.*

At 1:45 p.m. I balanced my checkbook. I realized that I couldn't pay my bills, though, because I left my personal checkbook at home. At 2:15 p.m. I called our veterinarian to schedule another appointment for our cat. She seems to be having a serious problem, even though she looks fine outwardly. At 2: 30 p.m. I looked into getting new business checks as my supply was running very low.

At 2:45 p.m. I realized (a little too late) that there could be a potential problem with the Ramsborg logo. I remembered that Holly had requested that I provide her with a QuickTime animation file on disk. I also remembered that she said she needed the QuickTime file to be compressed using the Apple DV-NTSC codec for her editing system, which I did. However, I realized that I had rendered the Ramsborg logo animation at NTSC D1 resolution, not NTSC DV resolution. Even though I did not render in fields, there was still a chance that the animation could be distorted, so I decided to re-render the animation at DV resolution and make a comparison. I quickly made the change to the animation project and then began re-rendering the logo.

While Ramsborg was rendering, I started work on the first of two Family Video Treasures (FVT) projects. I created a project folder, assigned a job number to the project, and created a timesheet. This is something I do for every project. I copied the images from the first CD that Geoff provided, and then began the process of modifying them to fit into the animation. The images needed to be scaled to fit within templates that I created for the animation. The templates added a white border around the images to give them a classic photographic look and also kept the resolution consistent. Speaking of resolution, it occurred to me that Geoff uses the same editing system that Holly of Immersion Inc. uses, so I checked the output resolution of my animation project. Previously I had saved animation files for Geoff using a different codec at D1 resolution. This had always worked before, but I wondered if the animation might be improved by creating it using the DV codec and resolution.

By 4:30 p.m. I finished working on the first FVT project, and it was ready to render. At the same time, the Ramsborg re-render process had finished. I compared the Ramsborg D1 animation to the Ramsborg DV animation and noticed a subtle difference.

The DV (720x480) animation file looked better. It appeared with the D1 (720x486) animation file, the QuickTime software had removed every 80th video scanline to make the animation fit DV resolution. I hadn't noticed it at first, but now that I had, it did not look so good. After briefly considering breaking into the FedEx drop-off box to retrieve the first CD, I decided that it probably wasn't worth the potential jail time. I would have to burn a new CD and create a new FedEx package to send to Chicago.

At 4:45 I decided to call Geoff at Family Video Treasures to verify that he was using the same codec that Holly was. At least, this new information could potentially benefit the FVT projects before they were rendered. Unfortunately, I could only get his voicemail, so I left a message. I had made previous attempts to create QuickTime files for Geoff using an older version of the DV codec, but I was not impressed with the results. It appeared that with recent updates to QuickTime, though, that Apple Computers had improved the DV codec immensely. I rendered some test frames to compare the animation with DV codec to animation frames previously rendered using the original codec. The DV frames looked better to me. If Geoff was still using the same system that Holly was using, then it made sense to use the DV codec for his projects as well. By 4:55, in order to continue moving forward with the project, I decided to render the first FVT animation using the DV codec. If it turned out that he still needed the original codec for his animation files, then I could always just re-render. I thought it was worth the risk.

At 5:00 p.m. I burned a new CD for the Ramsborg logo, created a new FedEx package for shipping, and then took the package to the drop-off box. After returning to the office, I sent an email and then called Holly to explain why she would be receiving two separate FedEx packages, and which one to use. Afterward, I drove over to pick up Rhonda from work, and then returned to the office.

At 6:00 p.m. I started the second FVT animation project, while Rhonda patiently worked on her own projects. By 6:30 p.m. I had the second FVT project rendering, also at DV resolution. With both of my workstations occupied, we packed up and left for home.

LESSONS/PROBLEMS

Well the DV versus D1 resolution issue has resurfaced again. This time I had to send a second FedEx package, because I had missed that issue on the first one. I think that becoming an expecting father has caused me to lose a few of my brain cells. I would have thought that nature would attempt to give parents more intelligence when they were expecting, but apparently it doesn't work that way. Fortunately, that realization allowed me to update another project for Family Video Treasures, so there was at least some immediate benefit from that. In the future, though, I will need to be a little more careful about this particular resolution issue before starting a project. Basically, I was able to accomplish most of my goals for the day, though, except for paying bills. Forgetting the checkbook prevented that. Again, I'm concerned that losing too many brain cells may be to blame.

PREDICTIONS

· *Finish work on the Family Video Treasures projects.*
· *Pay personal bills.*
· *Start APA CD packaging re-design.*

DIARY

At 8:30 a.m. I arrived at the office to discover a problem with the FVT projects. The first project apparently quit rendering very early in the animation. This did not thrill me, because I was still in the office yesterday when it apparently decided to quit. Also, on the second FVT project, the first 240 frames of the animation were rendered incorrectly for some reason. I decided to tackle the first project first.

My older, Tri-Star workstation seemed to have developed a problem with the first FVT animation for some reason. After several attempts, I could not get it to render more than one frame of animation for the project. Rebooting the machine made no difference. I was not sure what created this sudden, unhelpful attitude in my computer, but it did not make me happy. I decided to deal with that later, though, and copied all of the files from the Tri-Star to the newer Dell workstation.

It was now 9:30 a.m., and the Dell workstation seemed to be having problems of its own. After attempting to re-render the first frames of the first project on that machine, the system crashed. I rebooted the Dell as I tried to recall where I had put those chicken bones and voodoo dolls. Apparently my machines were cursed this morning. Fortunately, I did not have to resort to black magic to revive my Dell. It seemed to be rendering fine after the reboot, except that it still had a problem rendering the first 240 frames. There is some script text that is supposed to appear embossed on the cover of the photo album within the FVT animation. For some reason, this text looked flat. I have included a photo to show the problem. I was able to track the problem down to an apparent bug in Lightwave, version 7. The software was having problems dealing with an image sequence being used as a texture map for the book cover. I did some experimenting with the software and found a different way to achieve the same effect. This new texture map process seemed to be working fine. The second photo shows the corrected result. At 9:45 a.m., since the animation seemed to be working now, I started the first FVT animation render again. Also, since the first 240 frames of both animations are identical, I could use the frames from the first project to replace the frames of the second project. Still, it would take about six hours to finish the

Family Video
Treasures
animation
image
showing
render error

Family Video
Treasures
animation
image
showing
correct render

rendering for the minute and a half long animation.

With the Dell workstation rendering, I decided to test the revised animation files I made there on the Tri-Star workstation, as well. It still crashed, even with the new files. It looked like I might need to reinstall Lightwave on the Tri-Star machine to fix the problem. For now, I decided to move on to other projects.

At 10:15 a.m. I decided it might be fun to watch money flying out of my bank accounts, so I started paying bills. For some reason, it turned out to be depressing instead. Go figure. I put the paid bills out on the front desk for postal pickup.

At 12:30 p.m. I took a break for lunch. Geoff from Family Video Treasures returned my call from yesterday. He verified that he was indeed using the NTSC-DV codec for his editing system, so that risk paid off. I was glad I wouldn't have to re-render the animations in the original codec, especially with the problems my machines were having today. The Dell workstation continued to render away the first FVT project in DV resolution.

At 1:00 p.m. I did some online research into digital still cameras. I had been thinking about getting one for work for a while now, but couldn't justify the cost before. With the baby on the way, though, I suddenly had a brand new reason to get *one. Also, Rhonda told me that she wanted to buy one for my recent birthday, but wasn't sure which one I would want. Truthfully, I wasn't sure which one I wanted either, so that's why I started to do more research. There is a website address – http://www.dpreview.com/ – which proved to be invaluable in comparing cameras and researching features.*

At 3:00 p.m. I decided to drive to the bank to deposit a check I had received today from Magic Box Editorial. While I was there, I attempted to order business checks as well. My experience there was not especially comforting. The individual who was supposedly responsible for taking my order, left the office in the middle of the ordering process! Another individual scribbled my order on a scrap of paper, so the first individual could read it later, then she left to go to a meeting. I felt that I had been rushed through the process, and by the end of the process I still wasn't sure if the check order had actually happened. I returned to the office a little bewildered, and I called the branch office to complain.

By 4:00 p.m. the first FVT animation had completed rendering. I duplicated the first 240 frames into the second FVT animation directory, so that project was ready to go as well. I loaded the finished frames from the first project into QuickTime software and started the conversion of animation frames into a QuickTime movie file. While the computer was busy with that, I left to pick up Rhonda at her work. By the time we returned to the office, the conversion was finished. I then repeated the process with the second FVT animation project, while Rhonda took a nap.

By 5:30 p.m. Both projects had been converted and tested. They looked good, with no noticeable errors. I woke up Rhonda and we left for the evening. We grabbed a quick bite to eat and went to the hospital where my brother and sister-in-law had earlier today given birth to their baby girl. It won't be long for us now. We're just a couple of months away.

LESSONS/PROBLEMS

I'm not quite sure what caused the errors I had today with the FVT projects. Perhaps there was a power spike or brown-out yesterday that made the computers slightly upset. The computers are attached to battery backup systems, though, so I doubt that this is the case. It looks like a Lightwave re-installation may be necessary for one of my machines. The other machine, while it also originally acted a little flaky, appears to be working fine now. I managed to meet a couple of my goals today by paying bills and completing the FVT projects.

However, dealing with computer errors prevented me from starting on the APA CD project.

Some may ask why I do not simply render directly to QuickTime movie files and save the conversion time it takes to make a movie from the original, individually rendered, animation frames. The answer is a simple. If a render crashes in the middle of a frame-by-frame render, I can simply start rendering from the last frame that rendered before the crash. If a render crashes in the middle of a QuickTime movie render, I have to start all over from the very beginning, and I also risk the same problem happening again. When animation render times start getting up into the multiple hours range, this becomes an important issue to consider. As it was made apparent today, render crashes do happen, and QuickTime conversions don't take all that much time to do. It is also important to note that QuickTime software does a much better job of creating QuickTime movies than any other software. I suppose that's to be expected, though.

PREDICTIONS

- Burn CD for the Family Video Treasures projects.
- Try to resolve whether or not bank checks were actually ordered.
- Create invoices for FVT projects and Time Warner project.
- Call Immersion Inc.
- Start APA CD packaging re-design.

DIARY

The first thing I did today was burn a CD for Family Video Treasures. I checked email while that was working in the background. One email that I received was from Sue of the Water Education Foundation, a client that I haven't heard from in about two years. She emailed to let me know about a new project coming up that would involve some 3-D computer animation. Basically, the animation would show how water supplies can be contaminated and how they should be protected. This particular project applied to water supplies within Indian reservations in the western United States. She was looking for an estimate, but I had several questions for her before I could provide any numbers. I needed to speak with her, but would have to wait. Since she is based in California, it was still too early to call.

I received a call from Mark at Magic Box Editorial later in the morning. Apparently, he had spoken with Terry Burris regarding a final edit at 2:00 p.m. today for the Time Warner "eye want more" spot. He said the edit might require some graphics assistance, and wanted to let me know to be available. I also received a call from Jim of Health and Safety Corporation. This was another client that I hadn't heard from in years. He was looking to create a simple 3-D logo animation for an independent film project, which was going to be broadcast on PBS. He said he would fax me details.

At 11:30 a.m. I checked out the CD for Family Video Treasures. It looked good, so I created labels and finished packaging the CD. Around noon, I took a break for lunch and researched digital cameras again. There are a lot of considerations for picking out digital cameras these days.

At 1:30 p.m. I drove to the bank to clear up the check order and also to deposit a check received today from GC Films for the Jack Nicklaus Museum project. That payment arrived quickly. I love it when clients do that. At the bank, apparently the checks had been ordered, but I was still not impressed with how the whole thing was handled. I definitely want to consider moving to another bank. The cost of ordering checks was also outrageous. That will be the last set of checks that I order from them.

By 2:00 p.m. I was back in the office in time to meet with Terry about the Time Warner spot. I spent a little time in the edit, and made sure that Terry received one of the new and fashionable Blak Boxx T-shirts. By 2:30 p.m. I found myself working on the spot again, because some changes were needed. I had some good client interaction time by being involved once again with

Time Warner Cable "eye want more" images. (Note that the face images that originally appeared on the TV screens for these four images have been removed due to copyright issues.)

the edit, and I also helped a little with the art direction. By the end of the edit, Terry seemed happy with the final product. He even gave me a few potential leads for more business.

At 6:30 p.m. I contacted Sue from the Water Education Foundation. She let me know the due date for the project was mid July. I had a few questions for her regarding what exactly needed to be shown in the animation. She said she would have to get back to me some time next Tuesday.

LESSONS/PROBLEMS

The goals of today were offset a little bit because of the unexpected edit for the Time Warner project. I did manage to burn the FVT CD and figure out the banking issue. One very nice thing about today was that a couple of new projects materialized. That's always great news. The time spent on the Time Warner spot was also well worth it. I don't often work with clients in a prolonged setting like a video edit. Having a client sit in on a computer animation session, I know, would be about as exciting as watching paint dry. The final product is cool to view, but the process to get there is often a little boring to watch. Whenever I do get the chance to work directly with the client in a setting like today, though, it is always beneficial.

PREDICTIONS

- Create invoices for FVT projects.
- Take cat to the vet.
- Call Immersion Inc.
- Start APA CD packaging re-design.
- Call Kathy of Every Day People Make a Difference for feedback on their website project.

DIARY

At 9:00 a.m. I worked on producing a round button design for a non-profit group that I'm involved with. I had been working on this project at home for a while. After receiving approval from the rest of the group, this morning I sent in the order for 5000, three-inch buttons.

At 10:15 a.m. I created an invoice for Geoff of Family Video Treasures, for the wedding open projects I created earlier. At 10:30 a.m. I made a list of clients that should receive promotional T-shirts.

At 10:45 a.m. I began an image search for the APA CD design project for PMG Video. Stephanie Pino of PMG Video provided several images that I could use for the CD. I made the decision that the best way to handle the look of the new CD and keep the feel of a disk in a series, was to replace the photograph and colors used in the original CD design, but keep other element of the design. I found a decent image to use for the CD from the images that Stephanie made available, but it would need some modification in Photoshop.

At 11:30 a.m. I set up a project folder for the PMG – APA CD project. I called Susan Logsdon, who is coordinating the CD silk-screening process with the printer for this project, and then Mike Switzer, who is the agency contact for this project. In discussions with them I tried to get more information about the needs and limitations of the project. The last CD print

STEPHANIE PINO OF PMG VIDEO
COMMUNICATIONS INC.

project we worked on did not produce the results that we wanted, so we're using a new printer this time around. After talking with Mike and Susan, I was looking to create a design using one spot color and process black ink over a white ink background, so basically it was a three-color print project. Although I didn't know what text should appear on the CD design yet, I did at least have a good idea of a direction.

At 12:15 p.m. I had a working lunch. I pulled the folder from the last APA CD job to get more specifics about that job for reference. I looked at the old Pantone colors to try to select a new Pantone color for this new project. I accessed the archive CD for the previous project as well, to load up the old files onto the system again. This should save time in creating the new design.

At 1:15 p.m. I drove home to take our cat Nikki in for vaccines and to pick up new diet food and a new antibiotic that should be effective in treating her problems. While I was out, I received a call from Holly of Immersion Inc. Her client was very happy with the animation that I sent. That project was basically done, then, so I could invoice.

At 3:15 p.m. I dropped Nikki off at home again. When I got back in the car to drive to the office, I noticed that the voicemail indicator on my cel phone was flashing. I dialed voicemail to find out that I had received a call from Stephanie of PMG Video. She had called to let me know that Geoff of Family Video Treasures had stopped by the office to pick up the animation CD, but nobody could find it. I called Stephanie back, but Geoff had already left the office. I should have been wearing my cel phone, I suppose.

At 3:35 p.m. I made it back to the office and called Geoff. I left a message on his voicemail to let him know that I was back in the office and that he could stop by any time. I promised him a T-shirt to make the trip worthwhile.

At 4:15 p.m. I called Holly of Immersion Inc. to return her call. She was also not answering, so I left a voicemail for her. I promoted the T-shirts again there, too.

At 4:30 p.m. Blake of Magic Box stopped in my office with a Windows 2000 networking question. I tried to help, but it turned out that Blake knew more about that issue than I did. I left him to explore his own solution. Geoff of Family Video Treasures then called back. He would be stopping by soon.

Geoff came by the office at 4:45 p.m. and picked up the CD. I also gave him the invoice for the project and his fancy new Blak

Boxx T-shirt. He was in a hurry, so he thanked me and went on his way. Rhonda then called to let me know that she was leaving from work. I told her that I would probably be working later to make some progress on the APA CD.

At 5:00, I burned a DVD for PMG Video for a client of theirs. They supplied the files needed to burn the DVD. Afterward, I started work on the APA CD design.

The photo that I chose to use for the CD had to be scaled up somewhat to match the 300dpi minimum print resolution that the printer specified. Generally, I don't like to do that, and instead prefer the image to already be at that resolution, but I had limited images to choose from on this project. After scaling, I had to use Photoshop's cloning tool to fill in areas for the rest of the CD surface area. Then I created a new color gradient overlay for the CD. By 7:30 p.m. I had a reasonably good preliminary CD design. I decided to stay a little longer to continue research on a digital camera. By 9:30 I called it a night.

LESSONS/PROBLEMS
The goals of today were basically met. The only one I didn't get to do was to call Kathy from Everyday People Make a

Difference. Everything came together well today. The only mistake was missing Geoff from FVT when he first came to the office. I suppose I should wear my cel phone all the time during the workday. However, that still worked out, as he was able to collect his disk later today. I was also able then to see him face-to-face and offer a promotional T-shirt. Even the cat seems to be doing better today. Life is good.

PREDICTIONS

- Invoice for Ramsborg project.
- Create test image for APA CD.
- Interview pediatrician.

DIARY

This morning Rhonda and I carpooled together to work. I dropped her off at work and discovered that her school was planning a staff picnic at a local park after work today. They needed to make a map to get to the park, though. I told them I would make one for them. By 8:30 a.m. I arrived at the office and started work on the map. When I was finished, I faxed it over to them.

At 9:00 a.m. I checked through my email. Steve from PMG recommended that I take a look at a DVD authoring package from Ulead that allowed animated buttons in the DVD menus. I checked out their website for a while.

At 9:30 a.m. Greg from GC Films called with revisions to the Jack Nicklaus Museum project. His client wanted the time-lapse sequence to be shorter, and they wanted two panoramas removed from the sequence. He also needed a quote today.

ME WORKING ON THE JACK NICKLAUS MUSEUM PROJECT REVISIONS.

Since I knew I wanted Magic Box to handle this issue this time, I had to wait for them to show up and get an estimate from them. It should be relatively simple to make the changes and produce a new Beta SP tape. I told Greg I would call him back later with the numbers.

At 10:00 a.m. I worked on the APA CD design a bit more, then printed out a test image for review. I chose I nice medium green, somewhat subdued, for the spot color. It seemed to work well. It also happened to be one of the logo colors for a version of the

APA logo that I had seen before in their brochures. I figured they would like that. I emailed the CD design to all of the involved parties for approval.

I later spoke with Mark of Magic Box Editorial about the Jack Nicklaus Museum changes. We worked out an estimate, and then I called Greg at GC Films. He didn't answer, so I left a voicemail message for him with the estimate amount.

At 12:00 I took some time for a working lunch. In case Greg wanted to see a test of what the full three-screen sequence would look like, I decided to quickly make the changes to the After Effects project I had. I rendered a one-screen AVI movie that contained all three sections. If I needed it, then, I could show Greg and his client the look of the final presentation. I didn't expect to have to use it, but I thought it would be better to be prepared.

At 2:00 p.m. I drove over to Rhonda's work to pick her up for our pediatrician meeting. Baby stuff – that's my life. The meeting went well, and we felt very comfortable with the facility and the doctors that worked there. They were a definite contender for our baby doctor.

*By 3:45 p.m. I was back at the office. Greg Carter had called to
verify the voicemail message I had sent by leaving a voicemail
message of his own. He seemed fine with the estimate amount.
I called him back and got his voicemail again, so I left another
message explaining that I wanted to deliver the sequence on
videotape this time and not even bother with the CD-R delivery.
That really seemed like the best of all possible options for
everyone involved. He would be able to encode that tape into
an MPEG file on whatever system he chose then, and would
not be limited to one specific projection system. I know that I
certainly did not want to go through the process of converting
AVI to MPEG2 again, although I did not share that sentiment
with Greg.*

*After that call, I tested a digital camera belonging to PMG
Video. They use a Kodak camera, which I thought produced
fair-looking images. Outdoor shots looked great, but indoor
shots were fairly grainy in appearance. At 5:00 p.m. Greg
Carter called with approvals for the Beta SP delivery medium.
I promised a delivery date for next Tuesday. That would give
Mark at Magic Box plenty of time to squeeze this project into
his schedule.*

At 6:00 p.m. I left work for the day and picked up Rhonda from work. We spent the evening at the school picnic, which also involved a Kindergarten awards ceremony. It was very cute.

LESSONS/PROBLEMS

Today was kind of a light day, as far as work goes. The change in the Jack Nicklaus project was unexpected, but it was handled well I think. I was just glad that I didn't have to deal with AVI to MPEG conversion nightmares again. The solution that Mark and I came up with would work best in any case. The only problem I had was that I didn't get around to invoicing today. I need to be better about that.

PREDICTIONS

- Invoice for Ramsborg project.
- Pay bills.
- Balance checkbooks.
- Attempt to create an estimate for Water Education Foundation project.
- Make sure that Jack Nicklaus Museum project is revised today.

DIARY

At 9:00 a.m. I waded through a weekend's worth of email. I informed Mark at Magic Box that the Jack Nicklaus revisions budget had been approved, so he had a green light to start that project. At 9:30 a.m. I started work on a project for friends of the family. They had taken some portraits and liked their pose in one photograph, but liked the facial expressions from another. I told them I could combine the two. I scanned their original photographs into the computer. After a little bit of time in Photoshop, I had a good composite image to use for printing.

At 11:00 a.m. I created an invoice for the Ramsborg project. Then I balanced my personal checkbooks online. I noticed a weird entry in the online information that didn't look right. I made a note to ask Rhonda about it tonight. At 12:00 p.m. I *took a break for lunch. I searched on the web to find a gift for Rhonda for when our baby is born.*

At 1:00 p.m. I paid personal bills for a while. At 2:00 I balanced the business checkbook and paid business bills. Amazingly, today I received the business checks that I had ordered, so the timing of that worked out well. At 3:00 I prepared my May 2002 accounting information from a bank statement I received last Friday. By 3:30 p.m., the accounting information was ready, and I faxed a copy to my accountant.

At 4:00, I decided to run errands. I deposited checks in the banks and stopped by the post office to mail bills and to buy more stamps. At 4:30 I was back at the office. I called Holly at Immersion Inc. to discuss several things, but got her voicemail. I left a message.

At 4:40 I researched past projects for the Water Education Foundation to get a good idea of what they averaged from a budget standpoint. I also researched similar projects for the Ohio EPA. I had previously done 3-D work with the Water Education Foundation, but the budgets were a little better for the earlier projects than what I was working with now.

At 5:00 p.m. Holly of Immersion Inc. called. We had determined that the QuickTime movie with the DV resolution had worked best. We talked about our impending baby-consumed lives for a while. After the call, I returned to working on the Water Education Foundation estimate.

The project called for the construction of a complete, 3-D, virtual, tribal reservation with camera zooms into specific parts of the village to highlight them. The budget that Sue gave me did not seem to be adequate for this kind of detail, but I still tried to find solutions to this problem. One suggestion would be to show only the parts of the village, but not the whole village; and then I could model individual scenes rather than an entire village. A second suggestion would be to animate the project two-dimensionally in After Effects. This could bring the project more in line with the budget. These would be my recommendations to Sue for tomorrow. I also wanted to nail down exactly what parts of the village were going to be shown, and what needed to be animated there.

By 6:30 p.m. Magic Box had completed the Jack Nicklaus Museum revisions. I decided it was time to head home, but first I took some photos of the Blak Boxx T-shirt for the company website using PMG's digital camera.

LESSONS/PROBLEMS

I didn't complete all of my goals today. The Water Education Foundation project requires more detail from the client for a more accurate estimate. This type of project can easily become very complex, so it has to be preplanned very carefully or it could get out of control. Before I give out numbers, I like to make sure I have a fairly exact idea of what the client will receive. It's generally not a good idea to allow any vague concepts to guide a project unless the client has a very good budget and is willing to pay by the hour. Even then, it's not the best way to plan a computer animation. I try to avoid it. Otherwise, the day went pretty well. I was able to accomplish the rest of my goals and even add a couple more. Also Magic Box Editorial did a fine job with the revisions.

Left: Digital photo of the Blak Boxx T-shirt front for the website.

Right: Back of Blak Boxx T-shirt.

PREDICTIONS

· Call GC Films about finished tape.
· Continue work on an estimate for Water Education Foundation project.
· Fix weird online entry in personal checking account.

DIARY

At 7:30 a.m. I stopped by the local office supply store to buy envelopes. I also looked at the office chairs they had and checked out their prices. I'm trying to find a new chair for our home office at a good sale price, but I didn't find one today. At 8:00 I arrived at the office. I went through email, and then decided to look into the personal checking account issue. I called the bank about the odd entry in the online information. I had asked Rhonda about it last night, but she had no idea what it was. The bank gave me instructions on how to dispute the charge. Hugh Rich later called to see if I was interested in lunch with him and Scott Gowans. I said that it sounded good to me, and we decided to meet here at my office around noon.

At 9:50 a.m. I decided to call the local telephone directory company to do something about my Yellow Pages listing. For some reason, in the last book, they had misspelled my company name as "Blar Boxx Computer Graphics" and also had the wrong phone number. To further add to the comedy of confusion, they placed my company in the "Skin Care" category. I have been receiving a free (yet still unwanted) subscription to "Rosie" magazine since then. Yikes! I have been meaning to deal with this issue for a while. Today I decided to do something about it. I don't generally get any business from my Yellow Pages listing anyway, but recently a former client had a very difficult time trying to find my phone number, so I thought it would be worth correcting. I spoke with the Yellow Pages representative, and he informed me that my local phone company was to blame. I called the local service provider at 10:00 a.m. and informed them of the issue. The misspelling of the company name had indeed been their fault, and they promised to correct the issue immediately. However, the phone number and categorization errors were still the responsibility of the directory listing folks. I called them back at 10:15 a.m., but I reached a voicemail recording. I left a message on their voicemail thoroughly explaining the errors and who was at fault, and I requested that they return my call when they had made the corrections.

After that fun, I looked into that weird entry in my personal checking account again. I decided to call the merchant where the charge was placed. I noticed there was an earlier legitimate charge from that merchant, but the second charge was strange. After talking with them, it became apparent that the charge was a mistake. Apparently, they had swiped my check card twice. They faxed me receipts for the transactions. The first receipt was for my purchase, but some random guy I had never heard of signed the second receipt. We were able to determine that the cashier had made the error, and the receipts they faxed me would help in making the dispute case with the bank.

By the time I had finished all of that it was 12:00. Scott Gowans and Hugh Rich were already sitting in my office, so we left for lunch.

I returned to the office at 2:00 and then had a series of phone calls. First I called Greg at GC Films to let him know that the tape was finished. I created a VHS dub from the original Betacam SP tape at his request. At 2:15 p.m. Mark of Braver Films called with a Photoshop question. He wanted to do a batch image conversion using Photoshop. I had not done this in a while, so I said I would call him back. After reviewing the procedure, I called him back and walked him through the process. Everything worked fine. At 2:30 p.m. my accountant called and we talked about property and income tax issues for this year. At 3:15 p.m. Susan Logsdon called regarding the APA CD. We were still awaiting client approval on the art I had created. The choice to use three colors seemed to be moving forward, though. I asked her about specs for the printer, and she said she would have a contact name and number for me soon.

At 3:30 p.m. I created labels for the new Jack Nicklaus Museum tapes. The videotape templates were still acting funky for some reason. I had to do some searching to find the VHS video templates that I needed. After I found them, I was able to print labels for the VHS and Betacam SP tapes for a professional look.

At 4:30 p.m. I spoke with Sue from the Water Education Foundation. I told her the issues I was having trying to deliver a 3-D environment for the budget she had. She informed me, though, that there was probably more in the budget than she originally realized. Some parts of the project were costing less than originally planned, and she might be able to divert some of that money into the graphics budget. This was a relief to hear. We discussed the different approaches of either minimizing the amount of 3-D modeling for the project or creating the project in 2-D using After Effects. She was definitely leaning toward the 3-D, so the increased budget would help there. She also let me know about ten different problem areas for water protection that she wanted to highlight in the animation. This gave me a better idea of what needed to be created for the western tribal reservation environment. The budget that she had was still somewhat low for the amount of work that needed to be done, but it was better, at least. Around 5:00, I decided to close down the office and head home.

LESSONS/PROBLEMS

I was able to essentially complete all of my goals for today. I prepared the videotapes for GC Films to have them delivered tomorrow. I worked on the weird bank entry on my checking account. That has been a pain to deal with, but I'm almost there. I just need to fax materials to the bank to formally dispute the charge. I was also able to make some progress in the estimate for the Water Education Foundation. It looked like it would be a 3-D project, and the estimate would basically be everything they had in the graphics budget. It should be higher, but there's at least a possibility that more money will be found. I should get started on building the environment soon.

One extra that I was able to deal with today was the phone book listing for my company. If I had ever done any business through the yellow pages, I would probably have been more *concerned about the listing. I get most of my business through word of mouth and repeat business. However, since my company has moved around a bit in the ten years that it has been in existence, having an accurate listing can at least help long-lost clients find my company. That's a good thing to do.*

PREDICTIONS

- Deliver finished videotapes to GC Films.
- Send fax to the bank to dispute the problem entry in my checking account.
- Begin work on Water Education Foundation modeling.
- Pay estimated income taxes for second quarter.
- Invoice for Time Warner and Jack Nicklaus Museum projects.

DIARY

At 8:10 a.m. I called a courier service to have the Jack Nicklaus Museum tapes delivered to GC Films. I included a swanky Blak Boxx T-shirt in the package for Greg. Then I sent the fax that I had prepared yesterday to the bank to dispute the erroneous charge to my checking account.

Around 9:00 I decided to go through my email. In that mess of junk I discovered one that was actually useful – a message from Susan Logsdon. She had sent me the contact information for the printer we were going to use for the APA CD. I printed out the email to have a permanent copy and I saved the contact information in my MS Outlook contact list for later reference.

At 9:30 a.m. I worked on gathering together my estimated income tax materials. Estimated taxes were due by June 15th, so

I wanted to get those out today. I spent the next hour emptying my bank account to pay the federal, state and city taxes that were due, then I prepared the envelopes for the post office. I usually send these via certified mail, so that can keep track of them. The dollar amounts are high enough that I wouldn't want one to get lost.

By 10:30 a.m. I started working on invoicing, and I was certainly more motivated to get that done after paying estimated taxes. I printed out the forms and had invoices ready for the Time Warner project and the Jack Nicklaus Museum project by 11:00 a.m. I checked out by the front desk and the courier had already picked up the package for GC Films.

From 11:00 to 12:00 I found previous jobs for the Water Education Foundation in my CD job archives. I spent some time reviewing what assets I had that I could use for this new project. I loaded up several of the scenes into Lightwave to see how much work was involved in creating them. They were fairly complex, but my software and hardware had improved quite a bit since the last project I had done for them. When I had rendered the previous project for the Water Education Foundation, I remember it taking several days to complete all of the animations. The same animations I loaded into Lightwave today were rendering much faster. I could probably also make better use of After Effects to animate some parts of the new project.

At 12:00, I took a break for lunch. I continued my quest for the "perfect" digital camera. After a thorough search for the features that I thought were necessary, I came up with a list of cameras. I filtered that list to fit into my price range. Then I further narrowed the list by reading in-depth reviews of each camera on the list. From that I narrowed the choices down to one camera, the Canon Powershot S-30. Then I checked for the lowest prices I could find through the internet.

At 2:00, I drove to the post office to take care of the estimated tax payments. It took a little while to fill out all of the certified mail forms, but the added security made it worthwhile. I also mailed invoices while I was there.

At 3:45 p.m. I left the office to pick up Rhonda at her work. I drove back to the office, and then I left her with the car to run errands.

At 4:15 p.m. I started working on a procedure to generate the landscape that would be needed for the Water Education Foundation project. The landscape would basically just be a backdrop for the reservation village, but it had to be 3-D, and it had to look at least somewhat convincing. I own a specialized software package that is designed to create landscapes, called Bryce. I had not used it in a while, but I thought it might work well for this project. Bryce had several features that were very well suited for the creation of landscapes. The selection of procedural textures and bump maps was very good. Also the landscape generation tools were good for creating different features like mountains and plateaus. The real-time representation of the resulting landscape was also a great feature. The problem I was having with Bryce, though, was its interface. Bryce limited the image size that I could use for landscape generation to a very small area of the screen for some reason. The surface texturing process was also overly complex and non-intuitive. I thought that Bryce had many great features, but the interface design was too limiting, and it was becoming very frustrating. By 7:15 p.m. Rhonda had returned from her errands, so I closed down the office, and we left for home.

LESSONS/PROBLEMS

Today was a fairly productive day. I was able to accomplish everything that I had hoped to accomplish today, so I was very happy with that. The only problem area was with the Water Education Foundation project. I spent a lot of time using a piece of software that wasn't giving me the results I needed. By the time I left work today, I was fairly frustrated with the program. Since I am going to have to eventually import the resulting landscape into Lightwave 3D to animate it, I believe that using Lightwave to create the landscape might be a better idea. I will have to look into that tomorrow.

PREDICTIONS

- Continue work on the Water Education Foundation project. Find a good procedure to generate the landscape.
- Call printer regarding file requirements for the APA CD.
- Pay Bills.
- Research cost of digital cameras at local stores.

DIARY

In the morning, I looked up local stores that sell digital cameras on the web. Most of them opened at 10:00 a.m., so I would have to look into them later. At 9:00 a.m. I started working on a procedure to generate a western landscape using Lightwave. It looked like using a combination of Photoshop and Lightwave was going to be better and easier than using Bryce. Within Bryce, landscapes are basically created using a combination of image displacement mapping and procedural texturing. The image displacement map I could create, with a great deal more control, in Photoshop. The only thing I missed were the landscape-specific filters that I could apply to the image in Bryce. Photoshop didn't have any such filters, but I could at least work in layers, so I didn't have to worry about destroying earlier work. Once I had a test image created in Photoshop, I opened Lightwave and created a large rectangular

Top Left: Displacement map for landscape in progress for the Water Education Foundation project.

Top Right: Displacement map applied to 3-D mesh in Lightwave.

Right: Landscape with texture and bump map applied, atmospheric haze, and sky background.

mesh object. I loaded this object into the animation portion of Lightwave and applied the test image as a displacement map. It wasn't exactly real-time feedback, but it worked fairly well with no interface limitations. After a while, I was able to make changes in Photoshop and update the image in Lightwave fairly quickly. The 3D landscape started to take shape. The process was working. By 1:00 p.m. I had a pretty good start on the landscape I needed.

At 1:00 p.m. I took a break from creating mountains to pay bills and balance checkbooks. It wasn't quite as exciting, but *it needed to be done. Afterward, I decided to check out local stores for their digital camera prices. It looked like the local stores were selling the camera I wanted for about $40.00 more than what I would pay by purchasing it over the internet. When sales tax was added, the number went higher. It looked like the internet was the way to go for a camera purchase. I did at least get to hold the actual camera I wanted for the first time, which was a nice thing to be able to do. It seemed like it was well designed, although the array of buttons on the back was initially intimidating. I grabbed a sandwich on my way back to the office.*

By 2:00 p.m. I had returned to the office. Jim of Health and Safety Corporation called to let me know he was making a second attempt to send materials for the logos he needed. Apparently he had the wrong address last time. By 2:30, Jim stopped by the office. We caught up on events that had happened since the last project we did together, and then he showed me the logos for his current project. Since this was a film project for PBS, there wasn't a whole lot of money involved. He wanted to keep it simple – probably just 3-D, metallic text with a simple animated effect applied. I gave him a few options he could use, but he basically left it up to me. He had a very short deadline, though, so I had to work on it today.

At 3:00 p.m. I started work on the first film logo. I initially thought I could work in Photoshop, but I wasn't happy with the results. I decided to use Lightwave. First I had to re-create the logo in Adobe Illustrator, though, to make a clean vector art file that I could import into Lightwave's modeling module. The logo was basically just a single word using a Times Roman font, so it was easy to make in Illustrator. The resulting vector art I then imported into Lightwave. I gave it a bevel and extruded it to give it some dimension, then saved it. I also saved the bevel portion of the logo by itself. The saved 3-D object I then loaded into Lightwave's animation module to apply surfacing and lighting. Once I had the scene looking the way I wanted, I rendered two stills. The first was the full logo object, and the second was just the logo bevel positioned at the same location. Tomorrow, in After Effects, I would take those stills and apply the lighting effect to it. I should be able to finish the logo tomorrow morning.

At 4:00 p.m. I had to leave to pick up Rhonda at work. We had a prenatal doctor's appointment to go to at 4:30 p.m. on the other side of town. The countdown continues…

LESSONS/PROBLEMS

Today a new project with a very tight deadline prevented me from getting to most of my initial goals for the day. However, simple projects like these, with tight deadlines, are often easy and quick to produce, and they can be a good source of extra income while I'm working on a larger project.

I was happy that I was able to at least find a good procedure for generating the landscape for the Water Education Foundation project. That was now progressing nicely. Also I was able to pay bills and confirm my decision on a digital camera. My other goals would have to wait for tomorrow.

YOURS TRULY

SPECIALIZED PLATES FOR THE BBOXX-MOBILE. THIS IS HOW I FIND MY CAR IN CROWDED PARKING LOTS.

WIDE SHOT OF OUR OFFICE SPACE